WHOEVER SAID LIFE IS FAIR?

WHOEVER SAID LIFE IS FAIR?

SARA KAY COHEN

AN AUTHORS GUILD BACKINPRINT.COM EDITION

Whoever Said Life Is Fair?
A Guide to Growing Through Life's Injustices
All Rights Reserved © 1980, 2000 by SaraKay Cohen Smullens

AN AUTHORS GUILD BACKINPRINT.COM EDITION

Published by iUniverse.com, Inc.

For information address:
iUniverse.com, Inc.
620 North 48th Street, Suite 201
Lincoln, NE 68504-3467
www.iuniverse.com

Originally published by Scribners

ISBN: 0-595-13783-0

Printed in the United States of America

For Elisabeth and Kathyanne

ACKNOWLEDGMENT

There are those in my life whose love
and support have made all the difference—
in different ways, at different times,
each relationship special and unique.
I hope each knows
how deeply rooted are my thanks.

You wanted justice and there was none—
Only love.

—Archibald MacLeish, *JB*

My husband and I separated on October 31, 1975. It was Halloween. That August had been our eleventh anniversary.

The day of our separation is very foggy to me—but I remember that even though I dislike them, I went to the beauty salon, and the woman who cuts my hair commented that it must be a special occasion because she hardly ever saw me.

I think that I gave the children pizza for dinner. Elisabeth, my older daughter, was seven. Kathyanne, my younger, had just turned four. Their father and I told them in the best way we could about the changes that would take place in all of our lives. I can't remember if he left before or after the children were asleep. I do remember that I was wearing a purple dress and that before he left he told me I looked pretty.

Late that night when I knew no one could hear, I closed the door of my bedroom and went into the bathroom. I ran the water in the shower and turned on the faucets in the sink and began to scream. I don't remember much of what I screamed, but three words I do remember were: "It's not fair!" As I screamed, I realized that I sounded more like a wailing animal than a person, and I couldn't believe that the sobs and noises I heard were coming from me.

1

I don't know how long I screamed, but I do remember walking into the bedroom and picking up a photograph of the four of us sitting on the steps in front of our house. It was a photograph that my husband had used in campaign literature when he had run for public office. As I held it tightly I walked toward the window, thinking now, no longer screaming, "It's not fair. So many years and so much time and work."

I must have looked out of the window for several minutes before I heard another voice speak from inside, one that sounded more hopeful, more realistic, less self-pitying. "Whoever told you life is fair?" it said. "It's time to accept what is and move on—to know what you want and need and to begin to communicate that to the people in your life who matter. It's time to plan and work for a new chapter. To reach out to a new life. It's time to finish growing up."

I put the photograph back on the bureau.

"I'm going to try—try very hard—to do just that," I promised the pale, frightened face that stared back at me from the mirror.

Several days later, on one of many long walks I would be taking, I wandered into a favorite bookstore.

"Do you have any of Katherine Mansfield's short story collections?" I asked.

"No, but we do have the last journal she kept, the one that preceded her death. She kept a diary all her life, you know."

"No, I didn't know. I always loved her writing. How much is the journal?"

"It's a first edition, one edited by her husband following her death. It's thirty-five dollars."

I took the money from my wallet, knowing at the same time that I couldn't afford it.

Very late that night, after the children were asleep, I read Katherine Mansfield's journal. Her hope, her sensitivity, her love of life, despite physical and psychological pain, were a comfort to me. I decided that in order to handle the stress and frustration of my own life, I, too, would keep a journal, one in which I would record the steps in my journey toward a new life.

I vowed that when my loneliness and fears overwhelmed me, I would write—until I was sad and frightened and angry no longer. More important, I would write any truth I knew about fairness based on my own experience. I would ask myself important questions and answer them. If life wasn't fair, I was determined, through this journal, to discover how one could make it as fair as possible. The journal became my inner dialogue—my constant companion in the late hours when anxieties about my future would overwhelm me.

Though all entries were originally dated, I have reorganized the material for the purposes of this book, so dates are not included. But the first entry was made on November 14, 1975. And the last was made on November 11, 1978—one year after my divorce became final. Both asked the question "Whoever said life is fair?" But during the course of three years, as you will see, my response to this question changed.

❧ 1 ❧

Whoever said life is fair?

I think it was my parents and teachers. They told me that if I acted in a certain way, if I worked hard, I would be rewarded. And yet now I know that that's not the way it works.

As I write this, I think not only of my own situation but also of the couple in marital therapy, my clients, who sit in my office fifteen years after their wedding. He is now a successful surgeon, and she is a mother of three who, as happens so often, quit college in order to support her husband while he went through medical school.

She is crying as she speaks to me, explaining the reason for making the appointment, but hoping her husband will tell her she's wrong. "I have become my husband's housekeeper . . . his employee . . . his workhorse. I am no longer his wife. Perhaps, in his mind, I never was. I know he doesn't love me. I'm not sure when his feeling for me left him, and there's nothing I can do about it."

And as he responds, she looks toward the floor. "I liked you better the way you used to be—young and fresh. Of course I loved you and I wish I could get the feeling back, but it's just not there anymore. My love for you *is* gone. You're right."

As I look at the woman, my client, her face seems to

4

cry out, "I am humiliated. I have lost all dignity. I have done the best I could do. *Why have I not been treated more fairly?"*

When we come into the world, we have no choice over the political, socioeconomic, cultural, and psychological factors that will mold us. We have no choice about who our parents are. And if we marry, there are no guarantees for either person that if love or commitment are there, they will last.

I recall a friend's words: "When I was a child, I thought all men—and even all women—were created equal. Now I see that some people are born with more opportunity for love and success. They are born more equal than others."

My thoughts turn to my life before marriage, the values stressed within my home as I grew up and the life-style I was brought up to desire. For me, marriage and family had always been a priority. I remember my father, a deeply religious man whose personality was both stern and fun-loving, telling me from the time I was a little girl, that he was saving money so that I could have what he described as "your own very special wedding."

My mother, southern, charming, and very beautiful, explained that the world was difficult and that a woman who invested all her energies in her marriage would ensure herself happiness. "Just let your husband take care of you like Daddy takes care of me. Work hard for him, and let him handle everything."

Above all, both my parents stressed that being kind and fair and generous to others, even if it meant denying how you truly felt or what your basic and individual needs were, was the only way to live.

5

But there were other factors influencing my feeling about the only kind of life in which I could be happy. Because of my mother's ill health, I did not live with my parents between the ages of three and six. When I finally was able to join them once again, I was far too eager to please, to be their good and accommodating little girl. Though I didn't realize it until recently, I was to take this inordinate need to please to my marriage, replacing good girl with good wife.

I recalled the evening that I met my husband for the first time. We were both living in Washington and I was feeling happy and so lucky because I was about to be granted a full scholarship and living allowance by Catholic University, one that would enable me to begin my first year of graduate school. For me, our meeting was love at first sight. Or so I thought at the time.

I remember each detail of this first evening together: the way my husband appeared to me as I opened the door, the dress I wore, the Italian restaurant he chose, what we each ordered, and what we talked about. As the hours moved on, a thought kept flowing within: "You have a purpose to your life now. There is someone to love, someone to give to." When at the end of the evening he asked when he could see me again, I remember feeling that he could see me any time he wanted. It was as if I belonged to him, as if I were his to do with as he wished.

After our separation, the horror of my situation seemed insurmountable. For several years, I had been working as a family therapist, one who specialized in marital therapy. It was a field I had become interested and involved in while completing my graduate work at the University of Pennsylvania School of Social Work, one which helped earn money for us while my husband completed law school at the same university. As the years passed, my work was planned and developed to fit into the schedules of my husband and then later our children. I loved the field I had chosen and felt gratified by my clinical effectiveness. However, after the children were born, the main reason that I continued to work as hard as I did was that we needed the money.

But in no way was the income my practice produced sufficient to meet the expenses that lay ahead. For I would be learning in the months to follow that I was attempting to get a divorce in a no-alimony state, where there was neither a "no fault" divorce law nor a law to ensure an equal division of marital property. Also, the woman who earned any money took the risk of receiving far less child support. I had no savings, no one to lean on, and no divorce or property laws working in my favor. For the first time in my life, I realized in horror that I was truly alone. I was afraid to think about what lay before me. I loved to work hard, especially if it was for something I believed in or someone I loved. But to do battle with the man I had loved, the father of my children, was a prospect that sickened me. It was essential that somehow I find the strength to face what was to come.

✿ 2 ✿

I think of someone I once met when I vacationed at a quiet and lovely area in the Caribbean.

On the second day of my holiday, while I was relaxing near the ocean, my thoughts were interrupted by a man sitting with a nearby group. He called loudly, curtly to the native islander whose job it was to arrange chairs on the beach: "Hey, Mac, we'd like you to set up the same chairs for us tomorrow." I watched as he handed money to the man, one older than he, who stood with dignity, silently listening. Then I saw him turn to his group to explain laughingly, "He told me this morning that his name was McPherson. Any man with that name should be called Mac, don't you think?"

Soon after, I decided to walk to the hotel to be alone and enjoy a cup of coffee. Then, wanting one last swim before evening, I walked back toward the beach. I saw the islander, Mr. McPherson, as I approached a sandy area. There was a small bird in his hand, one with a damaged wing, which he was carefully tending. Directly above was a parachute guided by a small motorboat in the ocean—a ride that several people staying at the hotel took, one that I now saw could injure any birds that happened to fly into its path.

"The ride looked like such fun, Mr. McPherson. I hadn't even thought about the birds. You're kind to do this."

"The bird is one of God's creatures, as are we all."

"May I help?"

"Yes, if you fill this cup with water. I keep bread in my pocket. I'm sure he is hungry and frightened."

Soon the bird was hopping around somewhat haltingly and slowly eating some bread.

"Do you think he'll be all right?" I asked.

"We shall see," Mr. McPherson responded. "I take the wounded birds home after work and my wife and I tend them. Sometimes they are able to fly again; sometimes they grow ill and die."

Though I saw Mr. McPherson working on the beach during the rest of my holiday, he did not mention the bird. Nor did I. On the morning I was to leave the hotel, in my usual last-minute rush, I was putting my suitcase into the waiting taxi when I saw him walking toward me:

"I knew you'd want to know, Miss, the bird flew away this morning. He took some bread and honey and off he went—all well and free."

"I'm very glad."

"I have watched you on the beach. You didn't take the parachute ride. Perhaps seeing the bird spoiled your fun."

"The bird didn't spoil my fun, Mr. McPherson—I'm not brave enough for parachute rides. I want you to know that watching you and talking to you has taught me a lot."

9

I also wanted to tell Mr. McPherson that people like him made life richer. Yet the words remained unspoken. Instead, we shook hands. But there was something in his eyes that told me he understood what was unsaid, and perhaps, just perhaps, he found a similar message in my eyes.

Not until I watched Mr. McPherson slowly walk away did I even notice his limp, realizing for the first time that one of his legs was badly crippled. It was then that I truly understood and appreciated his compassion and why for him the magic of nature, of a bird in flight, was etched deeply in his heart.

✿ 3 ✿

If life isn't fair, what is it that keeps us going?

As I think of Mr. McPherson, I begin to see that it is one's feeling of self-worth, of inner dignity, that gives one strength even when faced with terrible pain or loss. And the more experience I have, the more I see that a feeling of dignity, and its reflection in the attitudes of others, is a major prerequisite to mental health and a feeling of well-being. Dignity gives meaning to our existence—assuring us that life is worth living, that, in spite of pain and disappointment, it is still possible to find joy.

History has shown that even conquered and en-slaved people can maintain their sense of self-worth—that is, if some time during their life one has ex-pressed it to them. Of all gifts perhaps it is the most priceless. Montaigne wrote: "My reason is not obliged to bow and scrape, that is for my knees." Only those who truly believe that no one will ever be lower than they—that there is no way to face their lives without humiliation or shame—will lose their hope and their will to live.

I remember a woman I will call Anna, with whom I worked while doing my graduate work at the Univer-sity of Pennsylvania. My field placement at that time was the Philadelphia Society to Protect Children, the agency that worked with families in which the chil-dren were abused or neglected.

Anna telephoned me one day, shrieking into the phone that I'd better get there fast because she was going to murder her four-month-old baby. There was terror in her voice: "You'd better get here and stop me. Why should we live? We have nothing any more—nothing!"

It was early December. The year was 1965. All around, the shops were preparing for Christmas. There seemed to be such bitter contrast between Anna's desperation and this joyous season. And yet it *was* winter and cold. In spite of the lights and carol-ing, there was a sense of despair and death in the dense December air.

I didn't know Philadelphia well at that time, and since I had five dollars, I took a cab to Anna's home. It wasn't really hers; it was rented and located in one of the poorest sections of Philadelphia. Anna made an at-

11

tempt to keep her home comfortable for her family, but the street on which she lived festered with uncollected garbage. And rats.

By the time I arrived, Anna had been drinking a great deal, but she managed to tell me what had happened. Her man had decided that he had had it, and had walked out that morning, saying that he would never come back to that hellhole again.

Anna screamed and moaned. Knowing that this time he meant business, she was overwhelmed by her poverty and her plight and she didn't know how she would continue to care for her children. She hadn't wanted the youngest, the one she now claimed she wanted to kill, but her lover had refused to allow an abortion—threatening that if she thought of destroying what he called "his seed," he was going to leave her.

"What am I going to do? What am I going to do?" Anna whimpered.

"Right now you're going to get some sleep," I said, "and then, when you wake up, we are both going to have some coffee and talk."

Anna curled up in the middle of her bed like a frightened child. I covered her with a light blanket and rocked her baby to sleep. Then I put on the coffee.

When Anna woke up, she felt better. She awakened with hope. She drank her coffee and rocked her baby once again. I could see that she was the kind of mother whose love could give her children the ability to hope, which in time would sustain them, too.

She smiled. "My kids and I are going to have Christmas this year," she said. "You'd better believe it! My kids and I are going to have Christmas." Anna

12

had enough inner resources to recover her strength and determination. No one was going to defeat her.

❦ 4 ❦

Whom have I known in a state devoid of dignity who felt no hope for fairness?

I think of clients who are helpless with old age, friends tormented with debilitating illness, the hopeless eyes of a prisoner I met early in my work. And I think of a little boy I knew and grew to love many years ago.

I will call him Stephen Meredith, though that isn't his real name. I first met Stephen when, as a graduate student at Catholic University, I worked for the Child Welfare Department in Washington, D.C. At that time, Stephen was ten years old and was living with his aunt and uncle. His aunt supported the family as a domestic worker. Her brother, paralyzed from the waist down, spent his days in a wheelchair in their apartment. Stephen's mother committed suicide when he was four years old after her husband deserted them. "He didn't want to be a father and told my sister again and again not to dare to get pregnant. But she wanted a baby so much that she stood up to him, thinking that in the end he'd change his mind and love his child. He kept telling her to get rid of it," Stephen's aunt would tell me as she spoke of the sister she missed so much, "but she just wouldn't."

Stephen's aunt had brought Stephen to a special unit in the D.C. Department of Welfare that had been set up to work with children who were bright but unmotivated. "He used to like school so much and all of a sudden he has stopped trying. He's gotten so skinny but just won't eat. It's like the child doesn't want to live anymore," she told me tearfully. "I hate ever to leave him, but I've got to work. I give him breakfast before I send him to school, and after school he's with my brother until I get home at about 6:30 and make supper for all of us."

After meeting his aunt, I began to see Stephen weekly. Our times together were Wednesday afternoons, and, though it was against agency rules, I would always take him to a nearby store that sold ice cream. Stephen's favorite flavor was chocolate marshmallow.

Several months passed before Stephen trusted me at all. Week after week he'd read or play games in my office, or silently eat his ice cream, telling me as little as possible. After six months I still had no idea why he suddenly had stopped eating and sleeping well or concentrating in school. Then one day as we were reading a book together in my office before going out for our weekly ice cream, he suddenly began to cry. "My uncle makes me touch him and it makes me sick," he told me. Then the ten-year-old child told me of the sexual abuse he had been enduring each afternoon as he waited for his aunt to come home from work.

When his explanation was completed, his terror began. "My uncle will beat me terrible if he knows I told you," he whispered.

Fortunately something could be done for Stephen. Psychiatric help was arranged immediately for him as well as his uncle. And a temporary foster home was found. I took Stephen to this home, one where he remained until his aunt planned a different living arrangement for the two of them. Just a few months before my marriage in the summer of 1964, I saw Stephen for the last time. We read and talked for almost an hour and then walked to our favorite ice cream store. There he told me that though he was sad, everything inside him felt OK. "I'm sorry you're going away," he explained, "but my aunt and I are OK now. And I won't forget all of our talks."

Fourteen years have passed since I have seen him, but I was not to forget our talks either.

✿ 5 ✿

But where does dignity begin?

I remember infants that I have seen and the differences between them. Some, from their first moment, are loved and valued as if they were royalty. I am smiling now as I remember the blond-haired, blue-eyed son of dear friends—a child born a day before Elisabeth—who at the age of two tottered around with an appearance so regal that he looked as if he should be wearing a velvet cloak. I loved to watch him clap his hands in joy each time he learned a new skill. And there was the first time he threw me a kiss—still a bit reserved but no longer frightened of my newness.

But life would not be fair to this regal, beloved toddler or to his parents. He would die at the age of three of tragic burns covering his body.

As I watch Elisabeth grow, I often miss him. One day I received the following letter, one which caused me to think of him and miss him even more. (The letter was written for my response in a weekly column I write in the Sunday *Philadelphia Inquirer*. Later on in this book, I speak of how this column began and of its importance in my struggle toward a new life.)

> I am writing for your help because I have an eight-year-old son who has a terminal illness. My husband and I know from his doctors that at best we will have him maybe two to four years. My husband and I go to see the social worker at my son's hospital and she has been very kind and helpful.
>
> But our son is our only son and only child, and my husband and I cannot believe that this is happening to him and to us. We are too old (fifty-three and fifty-eight) to have more children. We prayed to God for our son and after a long marriage we had him. My husband and I cry a lot and we are starting to lose our faith.
>
> We are hard-working people, and have been all our lives. We give to charity and have been good Christians. We don't have money but we own our home and work

16

hard to keep it right. Our savings were for our Jimmy's education and now we are going to lose him. Can you say anything that can help us?

I responded to the letter, one to which there is no real response, in the best way I could:

I don't think that there is anything that I could say to relieve the anguish you are feeling. I am very glad that you and your husband are working with the social worker at the hospital where your son is being treated.

I don't know if there is anything in life more horrible than a parent's knowing that his or her child is dying. It is against the laws of nature and fills us with unbearable pain and guilt. All of us, when we give birth, feel that our children will replace us. And when we find that our life will go on and they, so young and innocent, will not live much longer, our horror is indescribable.

You speak of the situation's being unfair. Most of us were raised to feel that if we treat others fairly, we in turn will be treated that way. But the reality is different. Life is often unbearably cruel, and kindnesses few and far between.

I read your letter to a former client with whom I worked during the year following the death of her only child, a daughter. She asked to share with you some of what she experienced at her own irreparable loss. She hopes her words will help:

When my daughter died, part of me died, too. I know it will never be alive again. To me, my daughter was all that was good, innocent, and pure in the world. She was only five and she was going to live beyond me and, I hoped, choose to give birth herself. It is so precious to give birth—to lose one's creation is sick, ugly, and tormenting.

17

And so when Sally died, part of me died. There was anger, and pain, and disbelief, and guilt. And then finally there was calm and acceptance. For our children are really only lent to us for a very short time. They each leave and go on to build their own lives—one in which parents become visitors.

Our dear, precious Sally never knew the joy of creating her own life and her own home. She died in my arms—so thin and tired, but very dearly loved. She left us much sooner than most children leave. But the years with her have enriched me beyond words and will live in my heart forever.

As I remember these letters, the tears start to come. But I think, I will not cry now. There is no time. I must continue to write. I realize that I am struggling with something and finding something out—*the state of dignity begins with love.* Everyone, in order to feel happy and secure, regardless of age, must know and feel love.

As I write this, I think about a lovely woman who showed me both love and wisdom when I was very young. I was fortunate to have met her, for I very much needed what she had to offer.

My father practiced Orthodox Judaism, which meant that he was most traditional in his religious observances. All matters involving food and use of time for prayer were carefully adhered to.

Though my mother's religious background was not nearly as defined as my father's, she followed his lead, yet with two very strong, most unorthodox, exceptions: (1) A true southerner, she maintained her passion for Maryland crabcakes (not appropriate food, according to Orthodox Jewish law), which she ate from a paper plate on our front porch (sometimes in the dead of winter), insisting to my sister and me that she was eating tuna fish, even after we wised up and realized that our tuna looked different from hers; and (2) she adored Christmas—its glitter, its wonder, its spirit.

Most other parents who were as orthodox as mine sent their children to a parochial school, one where they would meet others from homes with similar religious practices. My parents decided, however, that I would attend public school. Not long after, my mother decided it would be a good idea for me to join a Girl Scout troop that met in the area. "You're much too serious a child," she told me. "I worry about you. Playing with other children your age after school will help you to laugh more."

My mother was pregnant at the time and I was confident that she was carrying my sister (she was). I remember telling her not to worry: "Things are going to be much less lonely for me when I have a sister," I explained.

Except for having lots of trouble with things like rubbing two sticks together to make a fire and tying knots that wouldn't become easily loosened again, being a Girl Scout was fun. My only real problem came at Christmas time when our troop was invited to sing Christmas carols at a local Lutheran home for the aged. After the caroling, the residents were planning to entertain us with a Christmas party.

It was with trepidation that I asked my father's permission to participate in the caroling, as well as the party that would follow.

"It isn't appropriate for you to learn Christmas carols and participate in a Christmas party," said my

19

father vehemently when I showed him the invitation. "Hanging stockings with your mother and then leaving potato latkes [Yiddish for pancakes—a traditional Chanukah dish] for Santa Claus is questionable enough."

I decided not to tell him that I had already learned the carols—my mother and I listened to them together on the kitchen radio when my father wasn't home.

"I don't see any harm, Charles," my mother intervened.

"I'm sorry," my father said. "She may not go."

Though my father's feelings were very important to me, I did not want to be excluded from my friends' fun, and so I planned for the first time in my life to disobey him: to go to the party. Since I couldn't ask him for money to buy a gift for a resident of the home, as our scout leader had instructed, I decided to draw a picture instead—making it my gift.

On the day of the party, following the caroling, I was introduced to the resident of the home assigned to be my hostess, Miss Daisy Gilmore. Even more southern than my mother, Miss Gilmore had blue, blue eyes, a radiant smile, and beautiful white hair. As I look back I realize that she was wise as well as eccentric. And very sexy.

Upon meeting her, certain that God would momentarily be ending my time on earth for disobeying my father, I spoke quickly, explaining why my gift wasn't bought in a store. Then, in order to make my amends to God or perhaps to bargain a bit, I went into a detailed description of the magnificent bravery of Judah Maccabee, the legendary hero of Chanukah.

Miss Daisy Gilmore, who didn't have the faintest idea who Judah Maccabee was, listened patiently and then said kindly, "I do so love your picture. My gift for you isn't store-bought either." She then handed me two beautiful hand-sewn handkerchiefs, one peach and one mint green, each crocheted around the edges.

"I'm not going to be able to tell my parents that I was here or show them my present," I explained, feeling that since I hadn't been punished with death, I could soon anticipate disease, or fire, or flood, or all three.

"I learned from my finest and most ardent lover," said Miss Gilmore, in her deep southern drawl, "that one just cannot afford to tell everything to everybody. One who does can hurt oneself badly."

"But do you think God will punish me for disobeying my father?" I whispered, wondering at the same time what a lover was, but deciding not to ask.

"No, I promise He won't," was her quiet and dignified response.

My friend and I had our private Christmas for two more years. I always had a picture for her and she a lovely, handmade treasure for me—along with some marvelous stories about the men in her life, including her latest, "a mere boy of seventy."

When I was in the sixth grade, as our Girl Scout troop prepared for our annual party in the Lutheran home, our leader received a letter from Daisy Gilmore. In this letter she explained that she had become seriously ill and would be going to Chicago to spend her last holiday with a brother who lived there. Enclosed in this letter was a note for me:

My dear little friend, as I prepare for this Christmas, I am remembering our first together. And I chose as my last present for you to share what I know and believe: It isn't God who punishes people. We cause punishment to ourselves and we can, if we choose, hurt others badly. Do enjoy your world remembering that it is the love, trust, and respect between people, in spite of their differences or perhaps sometimes because of them, that brings meaning and richness to life.

I didn't go to the party that year either. My note was placed with two handmade handkerchiefs in the box that Daisy Gilmore had given me at our second Christmas party. And there they remain to this day, a treasured reminder of a well-loved confidante of childhood—of a long-ago friendship that seems as fresh as yesterday.

🕸 6 🕸

In addition to love, what else does one need to attain dignity?

There is perhaps nothing more shattering to one's dignity than being out of work or fearing that income will not be sufficient to meet one's basic needs. How can one maintain dignity in this society of welfare checks, government handouts, marginal and chronic unemployment, and the ravages of inflation? I'm beginning to see how many, in these extreme and deprived situations, try. There are drugs and alcohol for escape. And there is the cult of masculinity, including varying forms of violence and delinquency. I think of Jason, a client I worked with years ago in Washington, D.C. A delinquent who for years was in and out of prison, he would say to me, "Why should I work, why should I try? The rich just get richer and, man, I just get more stuck. So drugs, booze, and stealing make me feel good—why not feel good for a change?"

All of us need to feel capable of sustaining ourselves, to have some control over our environment. Frequently the physical and economic horror of poverty becomes so overwhelming that emotional illness is the result.

I worked with a boy named Jeff while I was on the staff of the Philadelphia Psychiatric Hospital in 1967. Jeff helped me to see how chronic unemployment, poverty, and lack of hope within a family take their emotional toll on all members. Some choose to retreat behind walls of silence, perhaps venturing out briefly but usually returning to the only safety they can trust—emotional isolation.

One spring morning a training psychiatrist at the hospital telephoned to ask if I would work as cotherapist with a resident physician to try to help Jeff and his family. Jeff, large and handsome—he looked like a sixteen-year-old Muhammad Ali—had been diagnosed schizophrenic. He had always been shy and quiet, but his psychosis, his break with reality, occurred on the day that his father quit his job. "Why should I break my back any more?" he screamed to his wife. "For what? We'll never get out of this hellhole." And she, furious and hopeless, went from room to room, ripping and tearing and throwing everything in sight.

Jeff, an only child, witnessed his parents' moment of horror, and from that point on, refused to speak or to look at anyone. Occasionally, he would shake his head appropriately in order to indicate yes or no.

During one session with Jeff and his family, about six months into the treatment process, Jeff's mother cried out to him, "Please, Jeff, talk to us—please stop shutting us out." She started to sob bitterly, as her husband sat in pained silence next to her. Jeff remained motionless, staring into space

Later that year, I stopped working at the Philadelphia Psychiatric Hospital. And on the last day of my work there, I was walking to my car, parked outside the patients' recreation room, when I felt a hand on my shoulder; I turned and saw Jeff, standing tall and straight. Did I really see a slight smile on his face, or was I imagining it?

Jeff, who appeared to feel and see nothing, touched me again on the shoulder and said, "Goodbye, Mrs. Cohen. You have been a nice doctor. It's nice here at the hospital—safe."

I wanted to respond but feared the emotion I felt at that moment would frighten Jeff and cause him to retreat behind his self-imposed wall. So instead I nodded and smiled.

He too smiled (this time I was sure of it) and I touched his hand—very lightly.

I think that Jeff heard my thank you, and then he turned slowly and walked away. Perhaps, in the safety of the hospital, he had finally begun to feel able to

24

cope with his environment and to start down the road to achieving a feeling of dignity.

As I look back I can understand Jeff's feelings of hopelessness all too well. After a particularly unpleasant meeting with my husband and our respective lawyers, I had a dream that spoke to me of my fears. In this dream I was on a train and feeling frightened because I was alone. I looked around for my husband but could not find him. As the train pulled out from the station, a gnawing feeling began in the pit of my stomach. When I realized that I didn't know where the train was going, real panic set in.

Our journey felt endless and I decided to take a walk. As I moved through the corridors of the train, I felt afraid of some of the people I saw—afraid they would not understand and like me, afraid they could sense my loneliness and vulnerability and could hurt me.

Finally I arrived at the front of the train and opened a small door, one leading to an outside deck. As the air began to feel refreshing, I decided to walk outside, but as I did I saw to my horror that my train was on a collision course: Another faster, massive train was coming swiftly toward us. There was no time either to protect myself or to alert anyone of the danger. "I don't want to die," I screamed into the night, as the larger and faster train moved toward us.

When the crash came, I was thrown outside, but I clung to the rail, hoping that the impact of the collision would not throw me to the tracks. Realizing that I was badly hurt, I tried to stand but was unable to. I realized then that I was covered with blood. I wanted to find help and to see how the other passengers were, but no part of me was able to move.

Terrified at my inability to move, I wondered at first if I was dead. And then I knew I wasn't. "No, you did not die," I said to myself. "Help will come. You are alive."

When I awoke from this dream, I put on the light and looked at the clock. It was 4:00 A.M. "You must try to be your own help," I thought. "But the legal hassles are endless; I have no control over my life. I cannot move ahead, leaving this behind me. No matter what I do or where I turn, I *cannot* help myself."

I tried once again to sleep, but could not, and I walked into the bathroom to get some water. I opened the medicine cabinet and reached for a bottle of sleeping pills, one that I had asked my internist to prescribe, but had never opened. "It would be easy just to take them all," I thought. "Then it would be all over, all the pain and torment, and I could finally have peace."

But then I slammed the cabinet shut, never touching the bottle, screaming angrily into the shaking mirror of my medicine cabinet, "Coward. You goddamn coward. Your children need you, and you're not a quitter. Enough self-pity. Enough."

❦ 7 ❦

Dignity also comes from accepting and being confident in what you are.

My grandmother loved to talk of the farm where she was born and to reminisce about brothers and sisters and a favorite aunt who died in childbirth at the age of twenty-four. She talked lovingly of parents, later killed in the pogroms, whom she left forever at age sixteen, and of her own longing for an education while growing up, an impossible dream for an impoverished girl.

Once, before preparing to light the Sabbath candles, she asked in a hushed tone if I would do her a favor.

"Anything, Bubbie" (Yiddish for grandmother).

"I would like to know how to write. Teach me to write my name."

She watched closely as I began to teach her. "Kate Goodman Sherman."

As much as my grandmother loved telling stories about her childhood, she loved to listen to my stories about school, friends, and just about anything else I chose to share. Whenever anything in my life troubled me and I would tell her about it, I would always feel better.

27

During such conversations, she would nod her head in rapt attention, drinking coffee or tea with a sugar cube in her mouth, sucking the coffee or tea through the cube. And she'd always explain that her way of drinking tea was not good manners—not something children lucky enough to be American-born should do.

There was another thing my grandmother insisted I not do. After finishing a rich cup of coffee, she would lift her saucer and drink the last drops that had fallen into it, enjoying herself immensely but insisting that it was a privilege of a different culture and not one I could share.

When I was young, she loved to rock me in her old comfortable rocking chair, the same one that I have used for my two daughters. And when she was old and dying, she returned to this chair. I remember how she would nod her head in the twilight—looking so wise and beautiful—as we would sit together silently for hours.

Once I asked her if she would tell me the purpose of life—why we were here. "The purpose, darling, is your journey" is the only response she made to my question. But she answered another. "There will come a time when all pain is eased. Do not be afraid of life without me. My love will be yours forever."

On the last day that I spent with her, when death was very close, she said, in Yiddish of course, "I'd give anything for a saucer of my good coffee to drink but promise me that you will never drink it that way." And she smiled bravely and reached for my hand. I tried to return her smile and promised as I clutched her hand. A few days later, she closed her eyes for the last time.

And now, in times of trouble or pain in my own life, I go into my kitchen, where her same containers for tea and coffee stand. And after brewing and enjoying some coffee, I look at the drops left in the saucer and I pick it up, remembering her words and feeling closer to her. But I don't drink from the saucer . . . because I promised.

And when my daughters are with me and see me remembering, I tell them what I know of their great-grandmother and the Lithuanian peasant village where she was raised. I tell them of her "old country" and her solitary journey to her new one and how good she was to me.

And I tell them that my love for her reaches beyond the stars.

❧ 8 ❧

It is not always easy to learn who we are.

I once knew a woman whose father died when she was eight. She missed him desperately because he was warm and kind and thoughtful. And as she looked back on her life, she realized that her mother had missed him as intensely.

After her father's death, her mother would cry for hours at a time and would often withdraw to her room and drink. After drinking, she became physically abusive to her daughter, her only child. She would beat her until her eyes were black or until the child could bear the pain no longer and would faint.

But this child had inner strength, a will to live, and great intelligence. Somehow she knew her mother was miserably unhappy and very sick. Sometimes the child would hang on to life with what felt like bleeding hands, but she was determined to make good friends and to complete her education, which she did. In her loneliest moments, she remembered sitting on her father's lap and being held lovingly, and this memory gave her strength.

In college she fell in love with a medical student, and they were married. At first the marriage seemed to work. But the young woman, so hungry, so starved for love and affection, could not bear the long hours that her husband had to be away from her because of the demands of his training and profession.

Because she felt lonely and rejected, she criticized him constantly. Often she found herself overwhelmed with rage, but she did not realize that her means of expressing it and her own insecurity were a threat to her marriage. In time, her husband met another woman more able to handle the demands of his career, and he divorced his first wife.

There were then five agonizingly lonely years for this woman. But her strength helped her, and she enrolled in graduate school and began to develop an interest in graphic design. In graduate school, she was introduced to a friend of one of her fellow students. After a long and careful courtship, they were married.

In this relationship, there was never the passion that she had shared with her first love, but there was heightened maturity and a conscious decision to be less demanding, less needy. During this time she also began therapy, in large part because of her desire to succeed in this marriage.

Yet the woman never felt that what her partner offered was rich or fulfilling enough, and at times she felt tormented by loneliness. In therapy, she realized that some of this pain had to do with childhood needs that were never fulfilled.

Her husband was a distant man, but not unkind. Yet the intense needs of his wife caused him to withdraw even further. He felt angry, guilty, and inadequate; she felt isolated and enraged. She requested that they seek marital therapy. He refused and asked for a divorce.

When the humiliation and trauma of this separation began to ease, the woman, now in her fifties, began to question whether marriage for her was a realistic expectation. She was unhappy at times, but she was able to find work that fulfilled her. She did not develop as completely professionally as she could have had she entered her field at a younger age, but she enjoyed her work and the people around her. She invested in friendships and shared time with those she enjoyed, realizing and accepting the fact that some days and many nights would be lonely. This was her reality.

For the first time in her life she was coming to terms with who she was, what her capacities were, and how she could make her life work for her. She knew and felt success rather than failure.

One might not call her happy, and yet on most days she experienced a sense of inner peace and honesty that had never been hers before.

๑ 9 ๑

Sometimes something completely unforeseen, and so unfair, will affect our work, our entire lives. But dwelling on what is good in ourselves can restore our dignity.

Recently I received the following letter:

I am the owner of a small but successful dairy farm. While I was driving my wife to do her shopping, a truck coming in the wrong lane hit us head-on. We were in the hospital for several months, but God was good to us. We're both alive and have each other—almost as before. My wife is perfectly OK—but I am paralyzed from the waist down. Fortunately, we had medical insurance and all bills are paid. Also, the farm can be run by my wife and an assistant if I supervise carefully. With the help of our minister, family, and some good friends, we're doing pretty well. The devotion of my wife has helped me to cope more than words can say. I am not an educated man and am from an especially poor family. I didn't marry until my late twenties, and my wife and I feel fortunate to have found each other. We have a good life together. Our love is deep.

Yet there still remains one area in my life that I'd like your help with, and that is why I'm writing. My wife and I have one son, a fine young person of sixteen, a boy who always respected my ability to do hard physical labor.

For me schooling was never important, and I'm afraid that my son will look down on me now. Not only can I no longer work hard physically, but there is so much basic knowledge that he is learning in school that I know nothing of. I do read whenever I can and my wife and I have good conversations about current events and also things like our relationship and what we learned growing up. My wife, son, and I enjoy our family life and have long talks about all we're lucky to share.

I know I'm a good man and a good father and husband and that I should feel more confident. Yet I'm afraid that the accident coupled with my lack of education could hurt my relationship with my son. It's not that he's ever indicated anything but love and respect for me. But I want to make sure that none of my inadequacies could cause him shame. Can you help me?

And I responded to a man who in many important ways was so blessed, a man whom the unforeseen in life had treated cruelly:

I received your letter, one that touched me deeply, soon after I had completed a wonderful book, *Max Perkins, Editor of Genius*, by A. Scott Berg. This book is the biography of Max Perkins, the legendary editor who discovered and nurtured the genius of many American writers, including F. Scott Fitzgerald, Thomas Wolfe, and Ernest Hemingway. What stood out to me as I read this book was that Perkins was the kind of man who would have brought sensitivity, kindness, and sincerity to whatever his life's work or his circumstances might have been.

From what you share of yourself in your letter, you too have these qualities. In addition, you have the richness of a fulfilling family life, one that I'm sure you've given much time and effort to build and maintain. Your letter surely indicates that you are a wise man, a man who knows what's important in life. And this wisdom is something that even the finest formal education cannot promise.

Further, I sense that your wisdom has been increased by your recent accident, as horrible as that experience must have been for you and your family. As I read your letter, I thought of a client I worked with two years ago following her radical mastectomy. In her words, "I see now that what's truly important in life reaches beyond what the body can do or what it looks like. Of course, I wish that cancer hadn't happened to me. Yet, my bout with sheer pain and terror has taught me how important love and respect are in one's life, and these are treasures I am blessed with."

As time passes, I hope you'll value your own qualities more and more, qualities that those who love you can only cherish more deeply as the years pass.

✿ 10 ✿

Is there something more that helps one to attain dignity?

Yes. And it was my clients who first helped me to see, to put into words—to understand: *What is also required is the development of ethics, standards, ideals, and an ability to assume responsibility, to set standards for oneself, and to live by them.*

I see often how children can be reared in a way that makes this type of development impossible. These children are allowed to indulge in adult pleasures. There are no limits set on their behavior. An eighteen-year-old client with whom I work because of her inability to complete anything successfully explains this kind of background: "Even as a child, I knew I ruled my parents. All requests, from clothes to my social life, were always mine for the asking. There was never a need to develop responsibility in order to gain my privileges. And now, ironically, everything I begin I seem unable to complete for myself. It is as if from deep within I still expect my parents to be handing all things, even my achievements, to me."

This is not to say that those who have developed ethics and ideals are not vulnerable. "I'm here," said a client, a handsome man in his late forties, "because I have fallen in love with another woman. And yet, as strange as it must sound, I also love my wife. I cannot hurt her and I don't know what to do. I must meet my responsibilities to my wife and children, but I need this other relationship. I need her to express and enjoy and share the intimacy and passion that I never knew I was capable of."

Another client, a very attractive woman also in her late forties, explains, "I never thought this could happen to me. In returning to complete my graduate work after leaving it for so many years of homemaking and child raising, I've become deeply involved with a professor in my department. I'm strongly attracted to this man, and yet I love my husband. The idea of acting in a way that shows disrespect to him or to the life that we've built hurts me a great deal. What can I do?"

In spite of their dilemmas, this man and woman were conducting their lives with dignity and, as important, cared very deeply about the dignity of others. How different in their personal ethics—in their ability to assume responsibility—they were from a man I later met.

One autumn I attended a professional conference in another city. One of the speakers was Carl Rogers, a therapist whose philosophy and humanity have had a deep effect on my life. After he spoke, a man approached me as I was leaving the auditorium and asked if I would have dinner with him that evening. I explained that I had other plans.

He persisted: "How about tomorrow night?"

"I'm not sure."

"Look, you can trust me. I am forty-three, unmarried, and I work in the city. I'm only asking you for your company at dinner. Are you staying in the hotel?"

"No, with friends."

"Can I reach you there? You can see if your plans work out for tomorrow night. . . . Look, trust me."

I didn't, but I wanted to. I gave him the number.

The next morning he called early and suggested dinner at the same restaurant where I had had lunch on the second day of my marriage—when there had been so many dreams. I felt unable to go back; it would hurt too much. Yet I knew it was time. A year had passed since my separation. The mourning period was over. The challenge of going back to that particular restaurant was the deciding factor. I agreed to meet him.

That evening I tried to enjoy a cocktail and ordered dinner. I spoke a little about my children, the kind of work I did, my separation.

My companion, however, wasn't listening. Finally I said, "I'm going back to my friends' home to pack. I'm leaving for Philadelphia in the morning."

"I have something very different in mind," he said, smiling, and then added, "Look, I had a lot of trouble sneaking out on my wife. Luckily, she isn't too bright. She thinks I'm working. You're not really angry and if you are, we'll take care of that for dessert," he leered.

I stood up.

"Hey, relax."

I left.

In the taxi, amidst my hunger pangs, I thought about the whole experience. My reaction was not the result of the fact that he was married; I certainly have had nice lunches and dinners and important friendships with married people—women and men. I reacted this way because this person was not the kind of man who wanted to hear women or to know them. What he enjoyed was to trick, use, and humiliate. On this particular evening, his wife was victim number one.

✥ 11 ✥

As I write, I see, too, that art, music, religion,
and the written word help us to remain in touch
with our dignity and help us to handle the pain
and hurt experienced in life.

I see that these creative activities and involvements provide pleasure as well as a means of expressing oneself. They provide a means to claim dignity and to escape mental and moral anguish, even disintegration. I am remembering a sentence I once spoke to a beloved: "You have your music, and I—I have my writing."

One evening last week I went to the home of a friend, a writer, who is challenged by her work and who is diligently perfecting her obvious talent. On the wall of her dining room was an intriguing portrait of a woman both delicate and earthy—young, but somehow hauntingly older than her years.

My friend, noticing my fascination, explained that the woman was her mother, soon after she had come to this country from Europe, while still in her teens.

After dinner I learned more about this woman, whose eyes seemed to contain pools of wisdom for one so young. My friend had an older sister born with cerebral palsy. The child's family was advised that she would neither function nor be able to care for herself in any way. Institutionalization was strongly recommended.

"But my mother couldn't—she just couldn't," my friend said. "She insisted that her older daughter live at home with her family where she could give her an abundant amount of her time and love. My sister was never treated as though she were sick or helpless. We always expected her to grow to her fullest potential and become self-sufficient. I couldn't say that we always had an easy time. But what family does? And we never gave up hope.

"My mother is dead now, but she lived to see her older daughter, in spite of an illness that is and will always be part of her life, grow into a competent and accomplished person, an artist—one who has used her work to reflect the challenges she has lived with each day of her life."

We were no longer in the dining room, but as my friend spoke, I could picture her mother as a young woman in a red velvet dress, a woman with a wonderful and rich laugh, young and vibrant, yet free from illusion. For a moment in my mind's eye she was no longer quiet, with her jet-black hair pulled back, as in her portrait; instead, her long hair was loose and she was dancing.

Then, a young mother, she was holding her baby close to her breast. And I could feel the resolve of one who willed her tears into determination and strength.

At that moment her portrait seemed to be a prediction. She was a woman destined to be cherished by her daughters, a woman who knew innately that each child is born with unique potential and splendor. And like her older daughter she, too, against great odds, was born to create and reveal beauty, to become an artist. Her canvas—the most precious and priceless—was human potential.

39

✿ 12 ✿

Communication also fosters dignity, both in others and in ourselves.

For without shared communication, the desire to invest in a relationship will disappear, as will the feeling of love. But some find communication far easier than others.

What are some of the statements I hear from clients every day?

> "My husband and I don't speak the same language. It's like I'm speaking Chinese and he's speaking Latin."
>
> "Though I love my father very much, I don't know how to talk to him."
>
> "Why in hell is it so difficult for all of us to hear and understand each other?"
>
> "The only safe topics in our house are weather and sports. When we try to talk about important things, like how we're getting along, things really go downhill."

Communication between people who are emotionally involved is not merely a matter of what is said but also of what is felt, meant, and understood by each individual. Naturally, each dialogue and every person are different, and only the person himself knows what he really means by the words he chooses.

But knowing—understanding—what is meant and felt isn't an easy task.

As a client explains, "When I'm not sure what I'm trying to say and feel either muddled or afraid to speak honestly, then of course my husband cannot begin to understand me either. How could he? Things become a real mess when even though I'm not saying what I mean, I know he is responding to something I certainly don't mean—something entirely inside himself. At that point, we become like two trains on different tracks. There is noise—a lot of it—but no understanding—no connection."

Or as another client says, "Sometimes I'm scared to death to hear what is being said. It's like if I dared to listen, my whole life could change and the thought of that terrifies me. Yet when my wife and I are able to listen and hear and touch, when real communication does happen, it's worth all the effort that we put into our relationship. It's magic."

Several illustrations of the difficulties, challenges, and complexities of communication—of words spoken and what a former teacher described as "the music behind them"—come to mind. In each of the dialogues that follow, I have tried to express, in italics following the actual dialogue, the true feelings that seem to me to be behind the spoken words.

An unmarried woman, twenty-eight, is in my office speaking of her relationship with her father, who has been widowed recently, and a very difficult conversation that she had with him—one that she feels she didn't handle well. The conversation took place in her apartment when she was dressing for a date and her father unexpectedly arrived.

41

"I'm surprised to see you. I didn't expect you and I'm going out." *Of all the times for a visit. I really needed an hour for myself to get ready but I don't want to be rude. You look so sad.*

"I'm here because I know something's wrong. I don't enjoy anything any more." *Now that my wife is dead, I see no reason to go on. No one can take her place. I just want to join her.*

"Don't be silly. Look at you—you're healthy; you're active; you're still working. Why don't you call a friend and arrange to meet for dinner?" *I know you're unhappy, but if I tell you I know, we'll just both cry. And I'm afraid you'll shift the burden of keeping you happy on me—just like you did to Mother. For the first time in my life I'm starting to respond to a man—beginning to love him—and I'm afraid if I show how much I love you, I'll never be able to leave you.*

"I guess you're right." And, with a forced smile: "You get dressed. I've interrupted you. I'll call Uncle Harold for dinner." *She doesn't love me. She doesn't care. I am alone— so alone.*

In another situation a husband and wife were in my office discussing a separation. Each one wanted it for a different reason. The wife was hopeful that her husband would miss her and request a reconciliation. Her husband, however, wanted to use the period as a testing time to explore new relationships, remain in close contact with his children, and ultimately divorce. As our hour together began, she was crying. The husband reacted this way:

"Look, honey, if you're so upset, you can go out of state and get a divorce quickly. I don't want our time apart, when you know I'll be with other women, to drive you crazy." *I want her off my back. I'm tired of trying. And if she goes out of state to get a divorce, the property and divorce laws can work more in my favor.*

"That's not what I want." *What is he trying to do to me? He knows that's not what I want.*

"Why in the hell are you crying? You know it drives me crazy." *Why can't you see I don't love you anymore and stop begging?*

"I don't know— Yes I do, but I can't say it. I just can't say it." *I am terrified and so hurt. You don't love me anymore. You don't desire me. I am alone.*

All of us have feelings of love, hurt, and anger that must be expressed in order that problems be resolved or that we face the truth. Unless the inevitable misunderstandings and anger between people who live together are recognized and dealt with openly, the result is constant friction or angry silence, a complete breakdown of communication.

There is a couple with whom I'm working who care very deeply about each other. Both have had unsuccessful first marriages and live in their own homes. They have not wanted to talk of marriage or living together, because though they care for each other, they have each learned to communicate in very different ways—ways that cause a great deal of friction between them.

A recent session together started with the woman, whom I'll call Ruth, expressing a great deal of resentment as her lover, whom I'll call Larry, attempted to listen; he was obviously finding her anger difficult to handle.

Ruth: "When Larry gives to me, it's with so many

43

strings that I become furious. He was going away on a business trip for several days and offered me his car. I was very happy at this because not having a car is tough and having it for a few days would make my life easier. But then, after offering it, he said, 'Of course, you're going to have to pick me up at the airport Friday afternoon.'

"Now, he *knows* I can't pick him up at the airport on Friday. I work, and then I have to pick the kids up at the sitter!"

At first Larry doesn't want to respond, but finally he says, "I don't know what you're getting so upset about. I wanted you to have the car, but I also wanted a ride home from the airport."

Ruth: "Well, if you wanted a ride home from the airport you should have said so instead of offering me something first. It seemed like you gave me a gift and then took it back."

Larry: "And it seems to me that you're very selfish, because if you wanted to pick me up you could. After all, haven't I picked you up several times at train stations?"

Ruth: "There you go keeping score. Everything you do for me you want to make sure you get back."

What is really happening between this couple? Larry was raised in a home where he could not ask directly for things he wanted. Instead he had to manipulate in order to get them. He once told me, "I was on the football team, but knew my parents wouldn't like it. So I'd change my clothes at somebody else's house, leaving everything there—equipment, uniform, etc. Once I came home with a broken nose. My parents were so out of it that they believed me when I said I ran into a door. If they'd known I was playing football, my mother would have become hysterical and my father would have broken my neck."

Ruth, on the other hand, was raised in a home where both parents were very aloof and rejecting. As a result, she is easily hurt and has learned, in order to get what she wants, to make a lot of noise and be very demanding about it. In her words, "If I hadn't screamed a hell of a lot, nobody would have heard anything I had to say."

Specifically then, this couple communicates, asking that important needs be met, in very different ways; ways that are sometimes exceptionally irritating to the other.

Are they incompatible? Can this problem be worked out between them?

Larry answered this best when he said, "I see that whether or not we make it depends a lot on our determination to change old ways, old patterns of communicating, and—just as important—it also depends on how deeply we can grow to love and respect each other: understanding our differences and how they developed and working to understand each other when situations that hurt and anger us arise."

The following letter was written by a younger person struggling to communicate with her parents. I responded to it with what I know to be true, offering her as much encouragement as I could to prepare for her adult life.

I'm eighteen years old and am very upset about a situation in my family. You see, I love to write and I find that the diary consisting of short stories and observations that I write in each night is a lot of fun for me and also when I'm upset about something, I feel better after I write about it. But my mother makes fun of this interest and tells me that what I need to learn are things like cooking and sewing, which I enjoy and already know how to do. And my father agrees with her, telling me that I'm wasting my time with what he calls "your adolescent effort."

A neighbor of mine, a well-educated and nice woman, encourages me, but my parents dislike her. They call her "a Bohemian" and say they don't understand why I like her. When I try to explain to them that she and I speak together of college, jobs, and the choices that lie ahead of me in my life, instead of trying to understand, they make as much fun of her and our happy talks together as they do of my writing.

Why are they so inconsiderate of my feelings? When I try to reason with them, why are they so mean, refusing to understand me? Can you help me to understand my situation at home a little better, or if not, at least write something that can help me.

And my response:

It's difficult for me to comment on your situation at home, as I really don't know the people involved or who is present in your home. I do know, however, that frequently people who act insensitively toward another's feelings and attitudes do so because they're threatened—threatened because the person they ridicule is touching a part of them that they're insecure or unhappy about.

You sound as if you are a thoughtful person, who is very much in touch with her needs, and I was moved by the sincerity of your letter. I'd like to share a story with you, one that I hope you will find helpful.

There was once a child with a chronically ill mother who had asked her sister, whom we will call Beatrice, to care for the little girl. It was a strange arrangement, as the two sisters didn't like or understand one another.

The mother, ordered and controlled, found it difficult to laugh and enjoy life. Her sister, Beatrice, artistic and expressive, laughed easily and enjoyed life immensely. Her deepest love was an author, a young man who was beginning to achieve modest but definite success. One day when the mother entered the hospital, the child was brought to Beatrice's home by her father. And when he left her, the girl began to cry.

"I know you are sad and frightened," Beatrice said, touching the child's cheek. "Write about your feelings. You will see that it will help you."

And the child wrote a poem called "The Wheel," about her fear that her life would never again be happy.

When Beatrice read the child's work, she was very moved and suggested that her niece share it with her teacher. But the child refused, explaining that the teacher might show it to some who wouldn't understand and would laugh at her. "Please—you keep it," she begged her aunt.

"Of course," promised Beatrice. "It is a very lovely and special gift."

When the child's mother recovered, she and her husband came for their daughter. As Beatrice prepared tea, the child overheard her mother ask her husband if he had noticed the red slip that her sister was wearing. "Honestly, I've never seen anything like it; that is, of course, on a respectable woman."

"Aunt Bea was very nice to me," the girl said. But no one heard her.

Beatrice's lover died suddenly and her mourning was deep. Finally she decided to leave home, explaining to her niece that she was going away to learn to love again.

Years passed and when Beatrice's niece was in college, she received an envelope mailed from Paris, one without a return address. In it was a poem written on faded lined paper in the hand of a ten-year-old child. With it was a brief note, "I'm sure by now you have learned that no one will laugh at you if you take yourself seriously. And now that you're ready to claim it, I return a gift I have cherished through the years. Enjoy life and laughter. I do think of you often and with my warmest love."

Finally, two clients speak to me of an experience that they shared with the wife's grandmother, whom both love deeply.

The woman was very ill and her family had been told by the doctor that she would die soon and should be hospitalized. She was a proud woman and a wise one. She realized that her days were numbered and that though she hated hospitals, it would be easier for her and her family if she followed the doctor's advice.

"I've decided to go to the hospital but I don't want to go in an ambulance." *It will be my last ride in the sunshine. I want to enjoy it.*

"We understand, Grandma. Ted and I will drive you." [They each touched her hand.] *We hear you. Your last ride will be a dignified one and you'll be with two who love you dearly.*

And so they got ready to go to the hospital. The grandmother packed a small bag and got her coat. "There is one more thing." With a smile, blinking back tears, she said,

"I know you're going to laugh at me but before we go, I want to make sure my desk is organized. I want to balance my checkbook and I want a Scotch on the rocks." *This has been my home for many years and I will leave it in order as I've kept it in order through the years.*

"You, dear one, are a funny lady. I'll pour the Scotch for all of us." *How strong and courageous you are. We will miss you terribly.*

After the desk was in order and the Scotch enjoyed, that last ride, requested, heard, respected, and responded to, was a sunny and dignified one.

And that last week in the hospital was not an unhappy one. For when death came, the woman knew that she had been heard and loved. She knew, too, that her home has been left as she wanted it: in order.

❦ 13 ❦

It is necessary, too, to learn that one cannot control a beloved.

I am thinking of an interview in my office this morning. The wife begins:

"I believe in sharing. I want to share and give. I just don't think you should control all the money I make, when I'm not even sure what you have."

49

"If you love me you'll trust me," the husband replies. "And I'll handle the money."

"But there are certain things I want to understand . . ."

"Like what?"

"I want to understand what the children will inherit and how the money is invested. I want a better understanding of the insurance policies. When you and the attorney set up a trust for the children, why wasn't I involved in the planning?"

"Why can't you just trust me and leave it to me?"

"It's not that I don't trust you. It's that I want to be involved in the planning. At the end of the month, I want to sit down with you and together pay the bills and know exactly what we have and what we don't."

"You just don't trust me, do you? You're the kind of woman who will never be satisfied. You really don't know how good you have it."

"If I don't give in, you'll just stop talking to me, but there is one more thing that I want you to hear— something important."

"Well, what is it?"

"I don't want to go to your parents' home for the holidays this year. If you like, we can go next year. But we have two children of our own, and I want this year's celebration to be at our home with each of us at the head of the table. I'd like your parents to join us here."

"They won't enjoy it that way, and neither will I. We're going to my parents' home and that's final."

"But—"

"We're going!"

❧ 14 ❧

*Sometimes dignity in marriage can best be
preserved when the partners separate before all
love dies—in order to work on their individual
problems and in order not to hurt each other any
more than they already have.*

A former client writes from a new home in New England:

As I think you remember (but in case you don't, I'll fill
you in), six years ago my husband and I came to see you
for marital therapy. At that point we had been married
for four years and had two young children. I desperately
wanted to make my marriage work. My husband did not.

Though he seemed concerned for my financial needs
and future life, it soon became apparent to me that he
only agreed to marriage counseling to ease his own conscience. He no longer felt he was in love with me. He
showed no concern for my emotional needs, a problem
we had always had.

You scheduled appointments with us together and also
saw us separately. I do not know what you and my husband spoke about during your individual sessions with
him, but I do remember, as if it were yesterday, certain
questions you asked when you and I or the three of us
were together.

You asked if I felt I had failed because my husband no
longer seemed to love me. As I examined this, I began to

51

see that I did feel like a failure. Yet, as I reflected, I realized that this perception of failure was very unfair to me. I began to value my fine qualities and to see that I *could* work very hard and do a great deal but I certainly *could not* force my partner to love and desire me. And I began to like myself enough to see that the loss was/his

The wonderful thing that happened is that I began to believe in myself as an adult woman with a capacity for enjoying life. I developed hope for the future, whatever it held for me.

As a result of counseling, my husband and I separated. I remember feeling, at the time of separation, that the marriage was over, and yet something told me that to divorce at that point would be a mistake.

It was during this separation that my husband really grew to appreciate me. For the first time in our relationship, he "courted" (an old-fashioned but wonderful word) and pursued me. He showed concern for my needs and feelings. I had never lost concern for his, but I saw that now that I could finally (and for the first time) appreciate my own needs and feelings, my own self-worth and dignity, my husband could also do so, and so could others.

After a year and half of separation, we reconciled and for the past five years have had what we both feel is a full, rich, and committed relationship.

We have left our life in Philadelphia behind us. My husband is teaching in Cambridge, and I am working on a master's degree in social work. Our children are well and growing.

It was in counseling that we both began to see that marriage is for adults, not children, and that the fulfillment that can be achieved between two partners who respect each other is more splendid and exciting than words can describe.

You once shared a definition of marriage, describing it

as a goal, an ideal, one that few realize completely but one that all of us can know moments of. We think of it again and again. "Marriage—the union of two who love and choose to live, grow, experience, and share together, respecting each other's individuality and differences while doing so."

I am very happy and wanted to share this with you.

❧ 15 ❧

And sometimes, in the long run, permanent separation is the best solution.

Another client writes from her home in Cincinnati:

The last time we met I was leaving for Cincinnati to begin a new life for me and my two children. As you know, my husband's falling in love with another woman and leaving us for her was devastating. And you know, too, that as months went on, the affair that I had begun had become too painful to endure. As I look back, I see that, at first, having a lover seemed a wonderful escape from my pain, a diversion. But because he was married, we couldn't have any regular plans. He saw me when he could fit me in. Though he said he needed me, he was protective of his wife's feelings. Nor would I ever see him on weekends. Though he claimed he loved me (and perhaps he did), I grew to feel that he was using me. And the relationship began to make me very depressed and unhappy.

I am writing to let you know that I'm a very lucky woman. In my new city I have a met a man in his late forties, just a few years older than I, who is also divorced and has learned from the mistakes of his former marriage.

We have taken time to get to know each other. We feel that we're compatible, and our children get along as well together as can be expected. Though we aren't exactly "The Brady Bunch," I am content. It's really nice to feel warm in bed every night once again.

I don't regret the affair that proved so painful while I lived in Philadelphia. My lover was like a transition. I met needs for him and he met needs for me. But counseling helped me to see I'm not blasé enough to sleep with a man one night without expecting him to care the next day.

Our work together also helped me believe that if I liked myself enough and maintained hope, love, real and obtainable, though certainly not perfect, could once again be part of my life.

◊ 16 ◊

Sometimes in arranging a better life, one of dignity and self-respect, it is necessary to learn to fight.

It is necessary to be heard and to be respected in order to live well. That means that sometimes, in order to make life fair for oneself, one must learn to fight. This is especially hard for a child who has been taught that fighting is always wrong. A client recently explained: "I hear the words of my mother ringing in my ear, 'You must never fight. You must always be good.' And so I've learned to take abuse again and again and never say that enough is enough!"

Driving through a small town in Pennsylvania, I noticed a beautiful young woman with long, flowing blond hair, dressed in blue and seated with her friends in front of a small apartment building. On her lap was a basket of flowers.

It wasn't until my car was very close that I noticed she was in a wheelchair. As I looked up from her wheelchair, our eyes met, and it seemed to me at that moment that her eyes were the most perceptive and caring I had ever encountered. I felt instantly that I had to stop the car and speak with her.

"Where are we going?" Elisabeth asked as I pulled the car over to the curb.

"There's somebody I want to talk with."

"But you don't know anybody here! Sometimes I don't understand you, Mommy."

"Me too, Mommy," piped in Kathyanne.

"Sometimes I don't understand me either but it's all going to make sense soon," I answered as I handed each of them a container of yogurt, half a peanut-butter sandwich, and a book—and crossed the street to approach the young woman in blue holding her basket of flowers.

She spoke first, her voice delicate but her perception stunning. "Hello, my name is Laura. I'm glad you stopped. I had a feeling you were going to when you drove by and I saw you notice my wheelchair. You feel stuck somewhere, don't you?"

I nodded.

"Why?" she insisted.

The words came slowly. "I'm in the middle of something very personal that I can't resolve in a decent way . . . no matter what I do and no matter where I turn."

As she spoke, her voice appeared reflective, far away: "In dealing with some situations, wars are necessary—the only language understood. Or you remain imprisoned, a cripple. I'm in a wheelchair but I'm not lame. I've refused to be. I've learned to fight."

I felt a lump in my throat and I could only nod. There had been those times when I questioned whether death would not be a welcome relief from my despair and fear. In the evening after the children were asleep, I would read certain verses of Emily Dickinson again and again, and when Julie Harris brought Dickinson to Philadelphia via *The Belle of Amherst*, I saw the play three times. For Emily Dickinson understood:

> *The Heart asks Pleasure—first—*
> *And then—Excuse from Pain—*
> *And then—those little Anodynes*
> *That deaden suffering—*
>
> *And then—to go to sleep—*
> *And then—if it should be*
> *The will of its Inquisitor*
> *The privilege to die—*

I was learning, as had she, that there could be some things worse than death—far worse:

Suspense—is hostiler than Death—
Death—tho'soever Broad,
Is just Death, and cannot increase—
Suspense—does not conclude—

But perishes to live anew—
But just anew to die—
Annihilation—plated fresh
With Immortality—

Again and again, more times than I remember, I had resolved and then written: "I will not die. It is not time. This hell will pass and until it does, I will cope. I will survive this—whatever it takes, I will not give up."

Now, as the months slowly passed, I was beginning to feel stronger. The mourning was passing and each time fear or despair overwhelmed me, or there was a legal setback, I forced myself to do something very nice for myself. I would invite a friend to dinner, take two hours and listen to music, or pack up the children and take them to a friend's house for a relaxing weekend.

I knew now that for mature and fulfilling happiness, a sense of self-esteem, a sense of inner dignity was essential. To reclaim or to find or develop this sense of dignity from within, when external pressures are great, demands the use of all one's strength and resources. But it is—with time and persistence—*always* possible. The beautiful woman sitting before me in the wheelchair was all the proof I could need.

When I returned to the car, the partially opened windows were finger-painted colorfully with boysenberry yogurt and peanut butter. And Kathyanne, the artist, called out cheerfully, "Do you know why we stopped, Mommy?"

"Yes, I had something to find out and found some-one who could help me."

"I love new friends," Elisabeth said, smiling.

Then the three of us drove for a while, talking and laughing until we found our kind of quaint store, and within it a lovely old figurine of a woman with a whimsical expression, dressed in blue and holding a basket of vegetables.

Our pretty lady now lives in our kitchen. And sometimes when it is late at night and I am alone drinking a cup of tea, the figurine appears trans-formed into a beautiful, vital young woman who un-derstands that one is truly crippled only if one accepts being crippled. And she knows, too, that to leave one's own physical or emotional prison requires a lot of effort and pain—and sometimes war.

But I hear her promise what I already know: that the pain will subside and that even before it does, there can be love and growth and sharing with friends— wonderful friends—old and new.

✎ 17 ✎

Often totally unfair and depleting situations occur within the context of work. Sometimes, to maintain self-respect in such situations, you must fight, even if it means putting your job on the line.

A friend of mine, a psychologist, worked at a hospital in the Philadelphia area, one designed to be a "teaching hospital." This means that interns and residents train there and are taught by more skilled practitioners how to perform the delicate art and science of psychotherapy.

My friend was a skilled clinician and family therapist. One day while walking through the wards, he saw a resident smacking and shaking a young psychotic patient. As the resident hit the patient, she screamed, "You must listen to me. You must not sit in silence. I am your doctor, and you must speak to me immediately." The resident and the patient were in a locked room, one my friend could not enter.

Unable to find the head of his department, my friend rapped on the door of the medical director of the hospital. This was a risky thing to do, as lines of communication in the hospital were clearly defined. Psychologists reported to psychologists, physicians to physicians, social workers to social workers, nurses to nurses, etc. But a very sick patient was in danger, and my friend knew it.

When he reported the scene he had just witnessed to the medical director, he was told, "This is a medical matter, and I will handle it." Two weeks passed, and my friend heard nothing. Strangely, the medical director seemed to grow distant, and when my friend tried to talk to him, he found him elusive.

Several weeks later, my friend again saw the resident mistreating the patient. But when he reported what he had seen to the medical director, he was told that if he wished to remain at the hospital he would say nothing more about the incident.

My friend loved his work, his wife was pregnant with their first child, and it would not be easy to find another job in an equally prestigious hospital. But he could not compromise what he believed in. He wrote a letter to the chairman of the board of the hospital, requesting an appointment. The letter was accompanied by letters of support from professionals on the staff—nurses, physicians, social workers, and psychologists. A week later he was informed by the medical director that his services were no longer required.

Looking back on his experience, he explained, "I put my job on the line, and I lost. But I left with my dignity intact, and with the belief that someday someone else would accomplish what I had left undone."

❧ 18 ❧

It can be extremely difficult to fight, to maintain one's feeling of dignity, when concentrated efforts are made to humiliate.

Dignity is a combination of pride and humility, a just knowledge and assessment of one's powers and limitations. To humiliate is to strip one of all vestiges of self-respect. Charismatic political and religious fanatics have destroyed relentlessly in this manner throughout history. When Hitler wanted to eliminate the Jews, he first had to remove all their dignity, all of their power to resist. His steps were devoted to gradually increasing humiliations, the removal of all rights, freedom of movement, and possessions. When all power and dignity were removed, resistance became psychologically impossible. As a result, over six million were led to their slaughter.

More recently, the world learned with horror of the mass suicide and murder that wiped out an American religious colony in Guyana, all followers of the Reverend Jim Jones, a once-respected religious leader. Despite Jones's words of love, equality, and brotherhood, as the events in the religious colony of Guyana unfolded and as the way of life within was revealed—the abusive treatment, the complete disregard for all feelings of self-respect—we realized, in horror, that the man whose followers called him "Dad" or "Father" was slowly stripping his "children" of all property, rights, and privileges—of all vestiges of dignity.

The crippling effect of humiliation is not merely a political weapon but also a personal one. During a conversation I had with a good friend, she explained why she has had so much difficulty developing confidence in herself and her ability to make a worthwhile life.

"As a child," she said, "I was raised to be completely dependent on my parents for everything. All accomplishments that were mine were put down. In fact, nothing I ever did seemed good enough. All endeavors were ridiculed.

"Ironically, I frequently did achieve a great deal, and I was viewed as a generally competent person. Yet I always had the feeling that without my parents' help I couldn't have done it. Also, there was an unspoken trust between my parents and me that anything I did for myself was always for them too.

"This treatment for so many important years resulted in an inordinate need to be cared for and approved of by others. During my adolescence, no longer wanting my parents to control me and angry at them for making me dependent on them for so long, I became a 'flower child,' looking for any strong figure, any guru, who could provide me with the right answers.

"Now, at long last, I am able to see that when you need to be cared for as much as I did, you walk a damn dangerous road. You can find someone to care for you, all right, but that person then has the power to take care of you in another way. He or she can kill you."

And a client recently spoke about the role that lack of confidence and emotional abuse played in her personal life.

"I am terribly unhappy in my marriage, but for so long I have been beaten down, humiliated, that I feel unable to hold my own in this relationship, to speak for my rights, to fight back."

When one lives in a state of constant humiliation, one loses the power to assert oneself and to fight. And frequently one loses the ability to understand and assess accurately what goes on in one's life.

✿ 19 ✿

One must struggle to keep one's dignity in humiliation, not to give in to feelings of shame.

Humiliation comes from the outside. It was Hitler who humiliated and degraded the Jews. It was Jim Jones who ordered mass suicide for his colonists.

But shame comes from within—it involves an insult or injury that exposes a real or imagined weakness. Shame can be explained by the client who said, "I have lost him. I am ashamed. I am a woman without a man. Without him I feel as if I am a zero, a nothing."

Or by the man who said, after working hard in a business for over twenty-five years and then losing it: "This was my father's business. He built it for me, and I failed. I failed his memory. And I failed my wife and my children. The idea that I did not have my father's strength and success and have not been able to provide for my family brings a feeling of shame that I cannot handle."

Each of us may feel shame to some degree at some time, but some groups are subject to far greater humiliation than others and so must fight even harder against shame. They must develop a pride in themselves and their origins, their nationality, ethnic group, or religion.

As I'm writing this I'm thinking of a young black client I worked with a few years ago who said, "Of course black is best—beautiful. We have to feel that way in order to survive. How long did you whites impose your standards on us? And how long has it caused us to suffer?"

And I think of Rita and how she embodied pride and humility. In spite of a lifetime of suffering, indignities, and ridicule, she never succumbed to a feeling of shame.

In the forties and fifties, when I was growing up, Baltimore was a city whose culture was a curious combination of both the North and the South. During this period, many white women hired black women whose chief responsibility was to care for their children. Their wages, if you could call them that, were pitifully low. But it was a job—one of the few kinds of work that offered any dignity at all to the uneducated black woman. When I was seven, my mother hired a woman to help care for my sister and me, and as was the custom of the day, we called her by her first name, Rita.

Rita was a very special lady. She was loving and kind and smart. Had a formal education been offered her, there is no telling what she could have achieved. But she could neither read nor write, and to my knowledge she never set foot in a schoolroom—except when she took me to mine.

It was against the law for Rita to walk into most stores, restrooms, and theaters in Baltimore (some movie houses made exceptions on certain days of the week, but then blacks were confined to the balcony). Public restrooms were marked "White Ladies" or "White Men." Those marked "Colored" were never cleaned and Rita would not enter them.

One warm summer day Rita took her nine-year-old daughter, Laverne, and me to a public park to play. We got thirsty, and I began to lead Laverne to the water fountain.

"Laverne can't drink there," Rita instructed.

"Why?"

"It's not for us colored."

"But there isn't one for her," I reasoned.

"So she'll have to be thirsty," Rita explained calmly.

"We're both thirsty," I said angrily, as Laverne and I walked hand in hand to the fountain. Before Rita could protest more strongly, a guard approached and pulled Laverne from the fountain. He started to shake her and she began to cry.

"Please let go of my friend. You're hurting her," I begged, pulling on his hand and arm.

"Little girls like you should drink with whites," he bellowed.

"Please," I continued begging.

"The hell I will," he screamed, and then he slapped Laverne in the face.

Furiously, I bit the guard on the hand and held on while Laverne ran away. And I refused to let go until Rita pulled me away—along with a hunk of his flesh.

On Fridays, on her way home, Rita would take me on the bus to my grandmother's house. At this time, though legally dead, the Jim Crow laws against blacks were still honored. We would sit at the back of the bus.

In our school, the term "Civil War" was never mentioned. Instead, we read about what was called "The War Between the States." "And believe me, children," explained my history teacher, a stern and frightening woman, "the South should have won!"

This teacher and I took a strong dislike to one another. And when, in our exam, I wrote that I wasn't sure who should have won but I didn't believe wars solved much, she gave me an F—with a note that I had become too big for my britches.

When I went home and showed my paper to Rita, along with a note that my parents were to come to school because of "your daughter's uncooperative attitude," Rita said, "Now don't you fret. That teacher might be schooled, honey, but she is very stupid. Grades depend on who's grading you, so today's don't matter none. Now let's just have a cup of hot chocolate, listen to some music, and talk about the whole thing after we relax a bit."

And Rita went to our old piano and played her blues, her spirituals, and, as always, "Old Black Joe" and "Dixie." When she finished playing on this day, however, Rita was not smiling her usual smile. She said, "I'm talking to you from my own learning and my own hurt. Dixie's my home now, Sugar, but promise me—even if they say you'll be ruined—promise me you won't ever allow yourself to be stripped of your pride, promise me you'll always believe in your ideals, in who you are and what you stand for." I promised.

Rita's greatest passions were her church and her music. Each year she'd invite me to her church's annual musical program. I'd sit next to Laverne and feel so happy hearing Rita's voice in the choir. It certainly was more beautiful than anyone else's. I loved her music-filled, spirited world.

Once I asked my parents to join us at the program. It was during the McCarthy scare; the Rosenbergs had just been electrocuted. My father, upset by my request, would only say, "Letting you go is risky enough. Don't you realize they might think we're Communists?" I didn't know who "they" were, but something told me that asking wouldn't help me understand any better.

I was a student at Goucher College, located in a suburb outside of Baltimore called Towson, when Laverne called. Rita had been struggling with cancer for three years and I heard dread in Laverne's voice: "She's at Johns Hopkins. It won't be long now, and she's asking to see you."

I said I'd be there soon, but it took me hours before I could face her—or was it my loss I couldn't face? On the way to the hospital, I thought about Rita's dignity, patience, and love and about how deeply our relationship had affected my life. It hurt me that someone

I loved so much had been forced to endure insult and humiliation all of her life.

The year was 1960. Goucher had just accepted two black students for the following September. The community of Towson was strictly segregated. All restaurants, theaters, beauty salons—even bowling alleys—were closed to blacks. During the summer of 1961, a Goucher College committee, one consisting of faculty and students, worked endlessly to persuade shop owners in the Towson area to change their policy. But by the end of the summer no real progress had been made. Rita knew of the letter we had mailed to all owners of public facilities in Towson, threatening a boycott if their policies didn't change. On the day it was mailed, I told her that we'd be able to have lunch together in a restaurant very soon. I know she wanted to believe me, but she didn't.

Finally, I arrived at Johns Hopkins Hospital and walked into Rita's room. She looked very beautiful.

"Rita, you're sitting up!"

"I've been waiting for you, child. You never saw me laying down yet, did you?"

We hugged for a very long time.

She died two days later.

By September 1962, all public facilities in Towson were integrated. But Rita, as usual, had been right. We never had our lunch together.

Years passed, and I eventually left Baltimore. My memory of those first years away returned a few months ago when I met a woman from the deep South whose husband's recent job change brought their family to Philadelphia. Their eleven-year-old daughter had been told by her teacher that in her new school she could not be called by her first and middle names—only by the first. When the child tried to explain that she didn't have a middle name, that Betty Ruth was her first name, her teacher called her insolent. "Why up North, if your name is longer or different, don't people take time to be nice and remember?" she asked her mother tearfully, explaining she wanted to go "back home, where more people took time to understand and everything wasn't so rushed."

I know that in the deepest sense one can never go home again. The home and people I knew no longer exist as they were then, except in my heart and mind. And home for me now is here with my daughters.

What is important, though, is that there's part of home, there's part of the South as I knew it, that will always live inside me. Wherever I am when "Yankee Doodle" is played, I know the words and I sing along—"for historical purposes"—but when I hear "Dixie," no matter where I am, in my heart I'm in my parents' living room and Rita is playing the piano. And I remember her telling me that the most important thing is to remember who you are and, in spite of the struggles and disappointments in life, not to ever let anybody take that from you.

✪ 20 ✪

What about the differences between men and women? Does one sex have an easier time achieving dignity than the other?

Myriad books have been written on this subject, and my life and my work have taught me so much about similarities and differences. But as I look back, certain recurring themes seem to stand out. When men come into treatment because of depression, it usually has to do with feelings of not being manly or successful enough. Women come into treatment asking, "Who am I? What is a woman really?"

It seems that the man suffers because he is ashamed of not being manly or potent enough—either in his work or in his personal life. The woman suffers when she feels inferior simply for being a woman, when she feels unlovable, or undesirable, or when she feels unable to reconcile her femininity with the demands of an increasingly competitive workaday world.

Many women feel deeply inadequate for the first time as they realize their children must someday leave them to claim their own life. "What will become of me when they don't need me anymore?" asks a young and competent wife and mother. "What am I trained to do?"

In times of difficulty, does the man who relates well to his family have an easier time? In times of personal loss, does the woman who has work and/or interests outside of her home have an easier time?

Yes, yes, yes.

One day a friend telephoned: "I just talked to an editor at the *Philadelphia Inquirer*. I think they're looking for the kind of column that you could write. Tell me when you have a few hours' break in your schedule so that you can arrange an appointment to see him."

"But I've never written professionally," I explained, remembering that doing so had been a dream, one buried long ago when other choices had been made.

"Haven't you ever wanted to?"

"Yes, but that was a long time ago."

As my friend was speaking, I thought back and I remembered . . .

In my first year in junior high school, a classmate who was very special and dear to all of us died of cancer. Her name was Gwynne Lee Gill, and when she died she was twelve years old.

Our English teacher, Mr. Velder, told us of Gwynne's death on a Tuesday. She had been out of school for five weeks. As he talked his voice kept cracking, and I saw him twisting his handkerchief in his hands. My seat was in the first row nearest the window, where I could see that Mr. Velder's shirt was frayed at the collar—as if that morning he hadn't cared how he looked. I was holding a yellow pencil and when he said Gwynne was dead, I cracked it in two.

It was with a combination of deep sadness and a sense of not understanding that her friends in Homeroom 215, Mr. Velder's homeroom, arranged a

71

memorial service. In our class yearbook, one written in memoriam to her, Gwynne was written about and the ceremony honoring her was reported. I remember as if it were yesterday how brave Gwynne's mother was during the ceremony, how hard she tried to control, then contain, her sobs.

Soon after Gwynne's death I began to write for a small creative-writing journal that Mr. Velder edited. He was very supportive of my work, especially a short story about the loss of my friend. This writing was a very important part of my three years before graduation.

On graduation day it was with tremendous surprise that I went to the stage to receive a special award in creative writing. I remember feeling pretty in a blue-and-white-checked crisp summer dress and hoping that my parents were proud. . . .

Holding the phone but not really hearing, I left my memories. My friend was talking—her words became clearer: "You've been so quiet. You must have been having one of your 'mind trips.' But as I was saying, I really think you can handle it. You'll grow with the job. I'm not suggesting it only because I know you need the money, but you have got to get out of your house once in a while and meet new people. You take care of your kids in the house, and you see your clients in your house. And in your work I know you feel it's unprofessional to socialize with your clients. For your own good, you've just got to try new things and get a change of scenery! I'm right, aren't I?"

"Yes, you are."

"Then when can I tell the editor that you are free to be interviewed?"

And so one of the happiest adventures of my life—a dream come true—was about to begin.

But can either sex ever have an easy time?
Of course not. Within each of us, male and female, are similar and differing needs. It is difficult to be a man, and it is difficult to be a woman. In other words, it is difficult to be human.

๑ 21 ๑

Dignity seems to have so many faces. It seems always to be changing.

Our challenge then is to hold to it as we dare to live and grow.

I remember the dignity of children I've seen as they've learned to master new skills. When Kathyanne first learned to finger-paint, she insisted that everyone, anyone, who came to the door of our house— friends, repairmen, the mailman—"Come sit here and I'll make you a picture."

And Elisabeth, as she learned to tie her shoes, would sit for hours at the bottom of the stairs practicing to perfection. In those days, her favorite request of anyone to whom such a question was applicable was, "Can I untie your shoes so that I can tie them?" I think of those days wistfully as now, Elisabeth, at age ten, has better things to do than tie her shoelaces. "They're boring tied," she's tried again and again to convince her unconvinced mother.

I think of the dignity of adolescents and teenagers who face the world ahead of them needing the support of their parents, wondering about the future. This is not an easy period of life, but for some it is easier than for others.

A very brave young person writes to me of a major concern in her life:

I am 17½ years old and very ashamed because my mother is in and out of psychiatric hospitals a whole lot. She's really a very kind and giving person. But she gets very depressed and sometimes feels so bad that she doesn't leave the house all day long. It upsets me a lot to see her that way, but I know that there's very little I can do.

She and my father have a very unhappy marriage and haven't been able to work out their problems. He doesn't pay much attention to her, and as I think back, he never really did. But I realize that their marital problems are theirs, and I can't really make it better for them. Yet sometimes I wish that they could have left each other because then maybe my mother would have had a better life.

But what's hurting me now a lot is that I don't know how to handle bringing friends to our house. In her pictures my mother looks as if she was once very pretty— but today she is sad and very overweight. She goes to a clinic, takes medicine, but still acts different from my friends' mothers. And I don't know how to explain her odd behavior to my friends. She's very kind to them when they come over, but I know that they think she's a little strange.

I'm sure you've met lots of people like her in the work that you do, so could you write a little something to me that can make my life easier. I care about what my friends think and also feel loving and protective toward a parent who tries so hard and suffers so much. She's given me and my brother and sister a great deal.

I respond:

It's obvious from your letter that your mother, regardless of the stress and difficulties in her life, has, in your words, given you a great deal. You're at a time in your life when other people's attitudes, especially those of your friends, hold much importance, and I can understand the discomfort you explain so well. In time, however, as you and your friends grow and as you continue to face your feelings about life honestly, I think that you will feel more comfortable about your situation.

As I read your letter I did think of someone I knew many years ago, and I hope that telling you about her will be helpful to you. This woman was a neighbor of mine as I was growing up in Baltimore. Her daughter and I were close friends. Though at that time I called the woman by her last name, now I think of her by her first, Rachel. I do this because she was then about the age I am now. And if I were to meet her today, I would hope that we could become friends.

I met Rachel when my friend moved to Baltimore when she was about ten years old, and she was a beautiful woman. But one thing I remember, even now, is that her eyes were very, very sad, and sometimes when she spoke she had a lot of trouble looking at you. For if her eyes met yours for too long, she would begin to cry.

Her two daughters felt strange and uncomfortable about their mother. My friend would tell me in whispered tones, "My mother's different. She doesn't have patience and sometimes I get so angry at her. I wish she were calmer and could sit with me and listen to what I have to tell her. And I can't stand the terrible fights between her and daddy."

As the years passed, Rachel grew apart from everyone. She would often remain in her darkened house for days and sometimes when I'd ask my friend how her mother was, she would just shrug her shoulders. At times like this, her eyes would resemble her mother's. And she would fight to hold back her tears.

Unlike me, my friend, in fact most of my friends, were very athletic. One of the things they all loved to do on a warm spring day was to jump rope double-dutch style— that is, with two ropes going at the same time—a feat that took a great deal of coordination. I would watch my friends jump in amazement, as I had not yet mastered jumping rope the regular way, much less double-dutch.

One day as I was watching, I heard a voice call to me from the house across the street. It was my friend's mother, Rachel. She was wearing a beautiful long robe— the color deep rose—and her long black hair was pulled back tightly.

"Sara Kay, I'd like to show you something," she said, her eyes smiling in a loving way, as she led me to her back yard. Once there I saw that Rachel had taken a rope and tied it to a tree so that one end was free for her to turn. She explained, "I've been watching you try to jump rope, and I'd be happy to teach you how. What you don't seem to understand is the little jump that is necessary before the big one. If you'll turn the rope for me, I'll show you."

And show me she did as she explained kindly, patiently, "Jumping rope is like life—you must be careful not to forget the little steps first."

Within twenty minutes I, so myopic that I couldn't possibly see the rope without my glasses, and so uncoordinated that my friends swore I had two left feet (I believed them!), had learned much more than how to jump rope.

I thanked Rachel in a very happy and excited way; before I ran to join my friends, she took my hand and said quietly, peacefully, looking straight into my eyes, "You've never been afraid of me, and you trusted me enough today to let me give you something. It is I who should thank you."

We both had tears in our eyes as she left the sunshine and walked alone toward her darkened house.

✿ 22 ✿

There is the dignity of growing maturity.

I am thinking now of two clients. The first is a woman who began therapy after the birth of her third child. After this third pregnancy, which had been unplanned, her body did not return to its initial tone and proportion. For the first time in her life, her breasts and stomach were no longer firm. In addition, she had very deep stretch marks on her breasts and abdomen.

"What has happened to my body just isn't fair. I can't stand to look at myself, and I'm sure my husband feels the same way," she explained during an initial interview. "Undressed, my body looks exactly like the Nile River—with all of its tributaries!"

By our last interview, however, her feelings about herself had changed considerably.

"I see now that what I have is a woman's body—no longer that of a young girl. I look the way I do because I have lived and I've come to accept and respect hat a lot. Of course, I also know that with a sensible diet and exercise I can once again feel more in control of the way I look. But for the first time in my life, since really thinking about what life's journey is, I don't want to turn the clock back and be twenty again. I now respect my body because it is a true indicator of what my life—my challenges, my struggles, and joys—has really been so far."

Another client, a woman who recently had a radical mastectomy, felt very vulnerable and refused to resume sex with her husband—fearing that her body would repel him. During our work together, she decided to share her concerns with him.

In her words: "For the first time since my mastectomy, we talked honestly and openly about my fears. What I learned from our conversation is that it was I—not he—who was repelled at the sight of my body. My husband assured me that it was me he loved—me as a complete woman. Of course he wished, as I wished, that I had not had this awful experience. And we realized together that both of us had a larger adjustment to make. But in no way did my surgery diminish his love and desire for me. And it didn't diminish his respect either.

"In fact, he told me that he cherished me more, because for the first time in our life together he realized that one's days are truly numbered and that the joys of the married life we have been lucky enough to share for fourteen years could end abruptly at any time."

✿ 23 ✿

Laughter, too, an ability to laugh at ourselves regardless of our feelings of pain or inadequacy, is a face of dignity.

One day, a man who doesn't live in Philadelphia and whom I don't know well, but to whom I was introduced through a mutual friend, called and invited me to dinner, explaining that he was in town unexpectedly. He suggested an unusually lovely restaurant and asked me to wear something elegant. It was a terrible period for me legally and I told him that I wasn't free to date. I'd have to bring a briefcase so that people would assume our dinner was purely business. He laughed.

The children had just gotten over the flu and I hadn't been out to dinner in ages. So being served a meal in a relaxed setting where somebody else would do the dishes seemed a lot more appealing than broiling the cheeseburgers that were waiting in my kitchen. As I arranged for a sitter, I dreamed of rack of

lamb, but decided that lamb would be too extrava-
gant. Instead, I would choose chicken.

At eight my dinner companion telephoned, "I'm
outside but can't find a place to park. Would you mind
meeting me?"

"Are you double-parked at the corner phone
booth?"

"No, I'm double-parked outside your house. I'm
calling from my car phone."

"Did I ever tell you I love rack of lamb?"

"Not that I recall. This is our first date, remember?"

When we arrived at the restaurant, the main room
was not filled. But the maître d' led us toward stairs
leading to the second floor. When I hesitated, my escort took my hand. "Come with me, lady with a briefcase." It was with a combination of reservation and
amusement that I decided to follow the maître d' and
my dinner companion. We walked through the empty
upstairs dining room to a small door which the maître
d' opened, and before me was a very charming room
with a table set for two. There were flowers, music,
and even a small love seat.

As soon as the maître d' left, I began to laugh, and
my companion observed correctly, "You're laughing at
me."

"Look," I explained, "this isn't the set of *Funny Girl*.
Here I am with my briefcase. I'm not sure that even
Omar Sharif himself could convince me to stay in this
room. I want to go downstairs and have my dinner, or
I want to go home."

As I spoke, I found myself beginning to yearn for
my cheeseburger, my kitchen—even the kids' and my
dirty dishes. My escort, definitely street-smart, con-

80

fided, "I've ordered rack of lamb and some very special wine."

"Good," I responded, "could you also request a doggy bag and a thermos? I'll be eating and drinking my part of dinner at home."

"Now look," my companion said in mock anger, "if you keep quiet for a minute I'll explain the reason for the room. I've never been married and probably never will be. But I've always wanted a home with a large private dining room—sort of a dream that will never come true. I work damn hard and have very little time to relax. So when I take time I'm good to myself. I pick restaurants that help me dream a little. Now you have my word that I'm a gentleman. My solemn word. So do I have your permission to order our drinks?"

I nodded.

Just before coffee, for no apparent reason, I started to laugh for the second time. "You're laughing at me again," teased my companion.

"Oh no," I responded. "This time I'm laughing at me."

"I see, and what will you be in the mood for after you finish?"

"You're going to be surprised when I tell you."

"No, Sugar, a guy like me has heard it all."

"OK. You're sure?"

"Yes—sure."

"Well . . . I want to see *Saturday Night Fever*."

"You what?!"

"You heard me."

"OK, lady—just one question. How many times have you seen it?"

"Tonight will make three."

81

After the movie, I suggested we say good night in the car, which was longer than the foyer of my home. And now it was my escort's turn to laugh uncontrollably, shaking his head as he did.

"Why are you laughing?" I asked as he kissed my hand and said good night.

"Lady with a briefcase, you're not my type but you're a hell of a trip."

"You're a hell of a trip, too. Thanks for a terrific evening."

As I got out of the car, I thought happily that in spite of everything, life could really be a lot of fun.

✻ 24 ✻

And dignity is never giving up.

Today I visited a hospital where a man was dying slowly of cancer. But when I asked how he was, he could smile, his eyes struggling to remain alive as long as possible. "I am fine," he said. "It is my body that is failing me."

I think of a special friend, a person who is ill, but who, though not well, was strong enough to deliver a paper at the annual American Psychological Association conference in San Francisco, which I attended.

Following the presentation of my friend's paper, we decided to celebrate his success by having a drink at a lounge with a panoramic view of San Francisco. As I took the elevator to join him, I struggled to sort out my feelings. I was so glad that he had been well enough to present his paper, but was deeply saddened by his illness. In the back of my mind I remembered, like a faded portrait, my one previous visit to this cocktail lounge—to celebrate my first wedding anniversary. On this day, twelve years later, I was in the process of divorce.

But the company of dear friends is always a comfort, and I knew the next few hours would be happy ones. As my friend and I were enjoying our lunch and getting a bit tipsy from the wine, we noticed a man and woman, each with very white hair, at a nearby table. At times they were deep in conversation and at other times they ate silently, enjoying the magnificent view—and each other.

They finished lunch before we did and as they passed our table, the wine having dulled any sense of my obvious intrusion, I asked, "How long have you been married?"

"Fifty-five years," was the husband's happy and kind reply.

"What's your secret?" asked my friend.

And the woman answered earnestly and with a twinkle in her lovely blue eyes, "There's no magic formula. Our marriage works because we've never stopped trying to communicate and understand each other. Through the years we have remained deep friends and we have worked very hard—sometimes against great odds—to keep it that way."

83

When they left, there were tears in my friend's eyes. "Some of us don't get the chance, do we?"

"No, some of us don't. I'm sorry you're ill. I will miss you terribly."

The next day, I left San Francisco and rented a car for a gorgeous and captivating seventeen-mile ride through the Carmel–Monterey area, on a magnificently sunny day.

During part of the ride I passed huge, secluded mansions with grandiose French names that in English meant something like "Pink Place on a Cliff" or "Our Enchanted Villa." Many of these estates are on hills, surrounded by gates, trees, and winding cliff roads, looking exactly like the castles in the fairy tales of our youth. As I drove I wondered how the families who lived within handled the snow—how they got their children to school—and I laughed to myself when I realized it *doesn't* snow here.

Then I passed a large, very rustic home. Though lovely, it didn't belong in a fairy tale. Its name made me stop my car and sit thinking for several minutes. The sign on the gate read "Wits' End."

During these moments of reflection, I wished that my friend could have been with me. I felt that together if we had knocked on the door, we would have met a family who understood that sometimes to cope and accept and endure in this world, in all of our lives, takes all of the strength we can find. Like the couple we had met at the restaurant, they would understand that to communicate and to care and not to give up even when the road ahead is rocky is a precious way to live and to build.

As I drove on, for a brief moment it was as if my

friend were with me. And I felt him touch my hand and heard him repeat a sentence spoken in a beautiful room with a panoramic view of a special city, "I shall miss you too, dearest friend. Always."

✿ 25 ✿

And there are the dignity and wisdom of old age.

A beautiful, wise, and sensitive friend shares with me her feelings about aging:

> Like so many modern women, it was in past years very important to me that my body be svelte and my hair the color it was in my twenties and early thirties.
>
> But as time passed I began to see that with the graying of my hair, there came wisdom. And there's something about the face that happens, too, as one ages. I've come to look at one's face as if it were a marvelous painting— one that could never be copied. Each line shows what a person has lived through and how he or she has coped with life.
>
> Are the frowns due to the difficulties of life? Or do they reflect the personality of one constantly bitter and angry? Are there laugh lines? Have the eyes remained kind and compassionate—that is, if they ever were—even though to live is to struggle?

Can the person, after the years of living that no book can tell you about, still look at you, meeting your eyes in truth as you talk together, and care about what you are saying?

And then there are the hands. They tell so much about how a life has been lived—by the way they are held and by the way they are felt and experienced. Do they reflect and appreciate art, love, and comfort? Can they touch and be touched with joy, honesty, and passion?

When I look at and touch someone's hands now or when I look into his or her eyes and see life's etchings on his or her face, I can see the past years unfolding, and I can sense the degree of kindness and integrity of the person who stands before me.

And when I look at myself in the mirror, no longer beautiful and young in the way I used to be so many years ago, I feel the dignity of the life and experience I have known—and I am happy and proud.

As I am thinking of what my friend has shared with me, two letters for my column arrive, incredible as they may seem, within days of each other:

A lot has been written in your column about marriage. I would just like to make a few comments. My wife and I have been married for thirty years. She is dearer to me than anyone else on this earth.

Our closeness and warmth through the years reflected itself in every possible way. She has been both my partner and my closest friend. Our sexual life was warm, rich, and mutually satisfying.

Five years ago my wife developed cancer and has had four major operations. At first she was very self-conscious about the scars on her body, but I hope that my love for her has helped her to cope with her disfigure-

86

ment. I feel that her illness has brought us even closer.

But my wife is a very sick woman, and when I'm honest with myself, which is difficult, I know that she is dying. She is in a lot of pain and is heavily medicated much of the time. I'm with her whenever I can be and comfort her in all possible ways. But much of the time she is resting or very ill.

In recent months, my wife has been too ill for any sexual sharing. And I am very discreetly having an affair with someone, never seeing her during the times when my wife needs me or is available for companionship. I sometimes feel very guilty about this. Yet my wife doesn't know, and my mistress has helped me meet some of my needs as well as endure the hideous pain and loss that I am feeling.

I respond:

Your honest and explicit letter says much about the love, conflicts, joys, and poignancy of a life shared with another person. Two days after receiving it, I received the one that follows. Though the latter was unsigned, the address on the envelope was the same as yours.

Could it be that, though you and your wife are each frightened to approach the other openly, you both are feeling the need to talk together about times shared—past and present—and these, the final days of your life together?

Two who have been as close for as many years deserve a private time to speak of dreams, realities, and fears—a private time to hold each other and say good-bye.

My husband is fifty years old, a young, productive, and vital man. We have had a long and happy marriage with great joy from our children and grandchildren.

I, too, am fifty years old, and I am dying of cancer. My body is mutilated from numerous surgeries. Yet through it all, I know that my husband is still in love with me, and this love has helped me to cling to life day after day. And believe me, during the past two years I have fought for every precious day of life—every conversation with my son or daughter, every morning that I awaken with my husband next to me.

Though my husband doesn't think I know it, about four months ago he began an affair. I think he sees this woman during the times that I'm resting or not expecting to be with him. How do I know? When a woman has been married as long as I have and has been as close to her partner, she can just tell.

I want my husband to know that I understand him and accept him completely. I believe that in choosing another woman now, he is both handling his fear of life without me and affirming that he must continue to live, even as he mourns what is inevitable.

I trust that the two of us have loved each other as dearly and honestly as two can love. I do not want the end to come. But I am very tired and there is part of me that can fight death no longer.

But I want my husband to know that I will love him deeply until our final parting, and that his presence has enriched my entire life—as I know mine has his.

❧ 26 ❧

*I see more than ever how important it is, in order
to achieve true dignity, to know and understand
oneself well.*

What I understand today that I had not in past years is
that when a person knows and understands himself,
the self-awareness encourages rich emotional growth.
And, as important, in relationships with others, those
who know themselves do not blame their friends or
loved ones for their failures. It is this ability to take responsibility for one's choices that makes deep, meaningful relationships possible.

Within each of us, there are feelings that pain us
and make us uncomfortable. Frequently we project
these feelings to the outside world, a world which in
itself is difficult to handle. The outside world becomes
less frightening when we find peace and acceptance
within. The process toward this awareness is never
easy, but it is essential to a good and productive life.

As Katherine Mansfield writes, "I want, by understanding myself, to understand others. I want to be all
that I am capable of becoming. . . . This all sounds
very strenuous and serious. But now that I have wres-
tled with it, it's no longer so."

✎ 27 ✎

Is pain in relationships avoidable?

No. There are two kinds of pain, however—avoidable and unavoidable. As we grow, as we change, as we face new challenges, some pain—often intense and terrible—is unavoidable.

But some is not. As a client, a young physician, explained, "I've always identified with the young doctor in Somerset Maugham's *Of Human Bondage.* Like him, I've sought women who would bring me only rejection and torment when I've offered love and acceptance. I'm finally learning that some situations and some relationships, as exciting as I used to find them, are bad for me, bring out the worst in me. Sure, in them I get very high—you know, those high highs—but I also get those low lows, and that's the pits. So now I'm building something new for myself. It's a state of being and living in between those high highs and low lows. It takes work to change, but I'm learning to stay away from the people and situations I'm allergic to—from interactions and surroundings that bring out the worst in me—and to choose others."

❧ 28 ❧

Sometimes even when love is deep and fulfilling,
two who love cannot plan a life together.

Several months before my divorce was final, a wonderful change came into my life. I fell in love. To love again, after so long, made my world joyful. "My heart is finally alive," I wrote in my journal. "It has been dead for so long."

But the relationship was one, regardless of how beautiful and special it made me feel, that could have been harmful to me legally. "Remember," my lawyer warned, "in seeing each other before your divorce is final, regardless of your discretion, you could be followed. And you're breaking the law. So do be careful."

We managed to see each other very often in spite of the difficulties. I was learning that it is one thing to love and another to love a person with whom one is compatible. It is the combination of love, respect, and compatibility that allows the formation of a good foundation on which a meaningful and enduring relationship can be built. When the latter is possible and a commitment can be made, then the real work begins. And it is work well worth the effort.

One evening when we had been laughing a lot, as lovers do, we decided that we would each speak of what we loved most about each other.

"I'll go first. That way you'll have time to think," he decided, smiling. "What I love best is how I feel with you and wanting then, because I'm happy, to give to you. When we're together I listen to, hear each of us. And as I put together all the moments we have and the depth of feelings they awaken, I am forever richer. I know you are also."

I had been listening, forgetting to think about my response. But it came spontaneously. "I love your eyes the best. I love the way you look at me, never afraid as our eyes meet. I love trusting that they will lead me to good and honest places."

Our relationship survived the hell of the divorce process. And during the most agonizing and terrifying months of my life, he was there—for which I am and will be always grateful. Yet different needs and demands in each of our lives caused us to leave each other.

On our last night together, he asked me if I thought I'd be all right.

"There are the children, my work, my friends. I'll be fine," I answered.

"I know you so well. Will that be enough? Can you be alone now after what we've shared?"

"I can be alone. I am richer now because of what we've shared. And, in these months, I have learned to be . . . to wait," I said gratefully, remembering the time in my life when I felt this prospect impossible. "And someday when it is right," I promised myself silently, "I know now I can trust enough to love again."

92

When he left, I cried. But the tears were not, as they had seemed before, forever.

❧ 29 ❧

It is very necessary, as we learn to maintain our dignity, to accept the inevitable aloneness of life—and the loneliness it entails.

In November 1977, I received the following letter.

I really need your help, for as I anticipate Christmas, though it is still several weeks away, my problem feels larger than life.

My divorce was recently final—it was a divorce that was very necessary, and I am relieved that the experience is behind me. Yet as relieved as I am, I am also in a state of disbelief. For in a million years I never felt divorce could be part of my life. Complicating my feelings are three children ranging in age from two to fourteen, and the fact that according to our divorce agreement my husband will have the three children with him during this Christmas holiday. I know that this is an equitable arrangement, and I do want the children to have a good relationship with their father. Yet the idea of spending the holidays without my children is very difficult for me, and I'm not sure I'll be able to handle the season well at all. I just don't want to let myself become sick with longing and self-pity, and yet I find myself in tears a lot as I think about Christmas without my children.

93

I'd appreciate your writing something that will help me put things into better perspective. I'd so like to be able to make my time away from my three children as pleasant as I can, and I'd like to be able to look back on Christmas 1978, and say, "It wasn't so bad after all." But though I wish I weren't, I am afraid.

I responded:

The most wrenching aspect of divorce, once two people have separated emotionally, is the fact that there are times when each must be separated from his children. A client, a man in his late thirties, echoed your sentiments during a recent session: "When I married I didn't know myself well at all, and I certainly had had limited experience of life. Yet I viewed divorce as something that could happen only to other people—never to me. That is the viewpoint both my former wife and I held as, in spite of our problems, we planned our family. This will be my first Christmas without my children, and just the idea of it leaves a fearful and gnawing feeling of loss in the pit of my stomach."

But it seems to me that your letter deals with a far larger challenge than handling the holidays without your children—it deals with how hard many find it to be alone, as well as how necessary overcoming this fear is to each of us.

It is, of course, so important to enjoy relationships with others. But it frequently takes a painful experience, such as the one you write about, to force us to recognize how very important it also is to learn to be alone. A friend spoke about this recently: "I was married right after college," she explained, "going literally from my father's home to my husband's. In my whole life there has been so little opportunity to be alone and to enjoy my own company. Sometimes now I do find myself longing for a few hours without the kids or without my husband. Yet after some time passes, I thank my lucky stars that somebody who needs me will soon be home again. I know that I dread the children's growing up, and I'm afraid that if my husband ever left me I'd crack up or something. Once in a while when he leaves the house angrily after we have an argument, I become just sick with the terror that he may not return and I'll then be alone, unable to manage my life and care for myself."

A former client who could have written the letter that you wrote so well and honestly, and who is working successfully to alleviate her fear of being alone, decided last year to keep a record of her first Christmas day and night without her children. When I received your letter, I asked permission to quote from her work:

"When my former husband picked up the children on Christmas Eve, I sent them off with a hug and a smile and then I went into my bedroom and had a good cry. After I allowed myself that, I vowed there would be no more tears. I also vowed that in spite of the lump in my throat, I would handle my fear alone.

"I felt pride in what I was able to do—just for me. The day before I had shopped at my neighborhood supermarket, where I bought the ingredients for a special meal, one I would love, and that my children, who prefer pizza and hot dogs to anything, would look at and say 'Yekk!!'

"So I dried my eyes, washed my face, and went downstairs to cook to my heart's content—for me. I even opened a half bottle of good wine, and a couple of hours later I put on some of my favorite music and sat down to a lovely and relaxing meal.

"I read late, and when sleep wouldn't come, I read still later.

95

"At about midnight, the tears came again and I allowed them—tears for all the dreams that hadn't come true.

"And the next day when I awakened, though my heart was a little sad, I felt stronger and more alive than I had in a long while. For the first time in my adult life, I truly believed that I was a woman who could handle being alone—a woman who didn't always have to be caring for others and who didn't constantly have to be needed in order to feel good—a woman who could take care of herself and be happy doing so.

When I finished writing this response, I remembered the day that I took off my wedding band for the first time in over ten years, placing it in a drawer, still hoping that the inevitable would not happen, that a reconciliation would be possible.

And I recalled the day so many months later when, after all furniture and household belongings had been divided, my husband requested additional books. In some ways, this experience was humorous. I said that all remaining books were mine, but I was told they were not. Since my name wasn't in them, I had no proof. And so I decided to part with all the books he had asked for.

On the day the books were picked up, I went into my bedroom and opened the drawer where my wedding band lay, reading the inscription on it one last time. Then I put the ring in an envelope and placed it on top of a novel, *Lord of the Flies*, which I had first read in college, not understanding it then as well as I do today. "Please take this, too," I said. "I have no need for it anymore."

Months before this closing of another final door—
one of many—I had begun to know and accept that life
is a solitary journey.

✿ 30 ✿

*As we struggle to be self-sufficient, we must not
miss the beauty of that which is the closest to us.*

Another letter brought this truth to mind:

> I have a small store in Philadelphia and was widowed
> three years ago. Ours was a mom and pop business, one
> my husband and I worked hard to build together. We
> were always very kind to our customers, our policy being
> "The customer is always right." I know that's good busi-
> ness, but even more, we cared about our customers.
> When I was widowed, I thought business would be
> hurt because my husband was the outgoing one. I'm
> doing fine though—much better than I thought. But
> sometimes I get very lonely in the store, missing his com-
> pany and remembering what we accomplished by work-
> ing hard through our years together. The customers miss
> him, too, and we talk about him. But what gets me is
> that, though I've been good to my friends and customers
> all of these years, not one person has ever invited me to
> his house for coffee or supper to help ease my loneliness.
> It's not that I'm looking for constant attention, just a

little more consideration toward an aging woman whose kids don't live in town and whose heart broke when her husband and best friend of forty-two years died.

Please don't advise me to go to social groups. I go to one every week, but that doesn't take the place of people who reach out spontaneously. Also, please don't talk down to me with things like "Develop your own confidence and then do more for others in order to get back." I have confidence and I've been doing nice things for people all of my life—cooking, inviting, and really caring! Now I want a little back.

Do you think anybody sees me, or are they blind to my need for friendship? Will I know somebody cares before I am too old to appreciate it? Because I'm alone and no longer young, have I become invisible? If there's anybody out there who does care, I'd like to know. If not, why not? Your comments please.

My response caused me to look into my own experience.

It is difficult to be alone and aging, and the loss of such a dear one in your life is something many can understand and relate to. I hope also that you realize the strength you show in your ability to continue to work effectively in spite of your loss.

You ask if people are blind or if you have become invisible. I feel that many people do see, understand, and care. But too few of us, because of the demands in our own lives, take the time to reach out, to be kind.

Reading and thinking about your letter caused me to do some soul searching and reflecting. As I thought how best to respond to your questions, I began also to think of a man I used to see in his corner shop, but never took the time to talk to. The loss was mine, for there was wisdom in his eyes.

When I first saw him, he was in his late sixties, looking out of the window as if waiting for someone to visit, to buy, or to talk. He looked old and tired, yet unwilling to give up hope or life. I often wondered about him, how he lived and cared for himself, for I rarely saw customers in his shop—an old shop badly in need of repair.

Though I promised myself many times that I would stop in to say hello, bringing some flowers, I never did.

Once I noticed that someone, most likely a student from one of the area schools nearby, had painted a portrait of him that sat, hauntingly proud, in his window. When I saw the painting, I wondered if perhaps artists allow time for observing, being, and sharing that the rest of us do not.

Finally, there was a sign on his door. It was written in red crayon in a shaky hand and read: "Store Closed—Sickness."

I found myself passing the shop more regularly; the sign was still there. I knew he had died when, about a month later, the crayoned sign had been replaced by a professionally printed "For Sale" sign nailed to the building which housed his shop.

You are right about how important it is to take the time to reach out to people who have touched us, while there is still time. And sadly, often we do not. But perhaps the saddest thing of all is that frequently we don't realize our folly, or how we can right it, until it is too late.

❧ 31 ❧

Frequently I relax in bookstores. Today I find that they are filled with books whose formulas promise happiness, fulfillment, and success. Can these formulas fulfill their promises?

There are no easy formulas or rules that can be applied to complicated life issues. No one can really tell another how to live and love meaningfully and effectively.

When I began my graduate work in 1963, one of my reasons for choosing my field was my own search for the answers that could lead toward a richer, more meaningful life. I felt sure that understanding personality development—how all of us function the way we do, why we choose what we choose—was a good beginning. I certainly believed that within my profession lay the secret to a more enriching life for myself and my clients.

But I soon began to see that this misconception caused much of life's disillusionment. There is no one answer for any of us. Though most of us are reared from childhood to believe that we will meet wise people who can answer our questions and solve our problems, this seldom proves true.

As one client explained: "One morning I woke up and realized that I had been living my life as if I were a programmed machine. I was doing all of the things that people said I should be doing; yet I was miserable. I have been so busy listening to other people that I have never faced my own needs—who I am. I used to look for answers, but I'm just beginning to find out what the questions are."

As we journey through life, a sign of maturity is the realization that no one holds answers for us. For the real key to our happiness and self-awareness is within each of us. Our challenge is to get to know ourselves, to ask ourselves what makes us what we are, to value our individuality, and to accept our inevitable flaws. With such perception we can grow, make our choices, handle our lives, develop our potential, and build relationships with others.

All of us fail, or feel that we do, as much as or more than we succeed—and frequently in the things that seem to be the most important. A client, in a first interview, recently told me that she was entering therapy because of her relationship with her son:

"Though I love him more than anything, our relationship is very bad. He is critical of everything I say and do. He has developed a terrible drug problem and has dropped out of law school. Where have I failed?"

Or, in the words of another:

"I gave so much to my business, and now I'm on the verge of bankruptcy. How do I tell my wife and kids what a failure I am?"

I cannot tell these clients how to handle their individual situations. It would be presumptuous even to try. What I can do, what psychotherapists are trained to do, is to help people to find the avenues within themselves, to know their options and use them to the best of their ability—as well as to understand any part that they had in creating their dilemmas.

All of us at times must pick up the pieces and get on with our lives the best way we can. But only we, as individuals, can choose the path that is right for us.

❦ 32 ❦

In the real world, there are no fairy tales.

The following letter represents a theme that has recurred many times in the mail I receive for my column.

> I am very much in love with my husband of six years. Ours was a love story out of a fairy tale. We met in college, fell in love, waited till graduation, and married. We have had four happy years and two wonderful daughters—ages one and four.
>
> But last year our fairy tale ended. Professional problems in my husband's office started weighing on him heavily. A bright and talented architect, he found that he just wasn't making enough money to make ends meet. Fortunately, with persistence things have improved. My husband is far less depressed now. Still, our recent year has jolted us, shattering our dreams of a perfect life together.

I guess I'm writing this partly to get some things down on paper. You see, I was raised to believe in fairy tales and now I see that in spite of deep love, if we approach marriage expecting to live happily ever after, we're in store for shattering disillusionments.

I'll find your comments or anything you can share from your experience on the subject of the jolt from a world of fantasy to one of reality most helpful.

I responded after reflecting on some of my own experiences. As I did so, I remembered a period in my own life when my daughters were the same ages as those of the woman who wrote.

Your letter is a realistic illustration that even those fortunate enough to find lasting love cannot predict what life may hold for them, their family, or their close and dear friends.

The fairy tales you speak of, those that promise happiness forever, can serve a very important function. In the words of a client during a recent interview: "My childhood was dominated by my parents' unhappy marriage and the poverty which intensified the emptiness of our lives. What got me through the hardest days of my youth was my dream of the bliss that could befall me in meeting my Prince Charming and expecting him to make everything better for me. I see today, however, the danger in not blending this fantasy with reality. For I know so well that my happiness, my success, depends on me—not a prince. And no words ring truer than those I heard recently, 'She who awaits her Prince Charming may have to kiss a lot of frogs. Then if she finds her prince, she may very well spend the rest of her days cleaning up after his horse.' "

For several years, early in my own marriage—before

divorce changed our lives—since my former husband's family was from New York, every winter his parents would arrange for a suite of rooms in a large hotel in Manhattan. At this time we would visit New York relatives. These were always happy days—or so I viewed them—days filled with warmth, laughter, theater, museums, and the mixing of people of all ages and varying experience.

My favorite was an elderly cousin, Ida. I think I loved her so much because in her dignity and wisdom she reminded me of my grandmother, who had died soon after the birth of my older daughter. Ida and I always had much to talk about. But once she startled me so early in my marriage when, sensing fears deep within me, fears that I never dared speak of and that I was sure I kept well hidden, she said, "My child, in the real world there are no fairy tales. And so many, too many, waste precious years pretending in order not to face and deal with the truth. Never let that happen to you. The truth, however painful, is as precious a part of life as love, and their combination is the only magic I know."

The hotel where we stayed during our winter holidays was the same hotel in which the Duke and Duchess of Windsor had an apartment. As it did so many others, the love story of this couple intrigued me. Perhaps my fascination was intensified because Wallis Simpson had grown up in Baltimore, as I had. As part of my work in undergraduate school, I had been involved in the plans for renovating an area near the heart of Baltimore where her childhood home was located.

One holiday season a few days before leaving for New York, I read that the duke and duchess would soon be leaving for Europe. In this article the duchess was quoted as saying that as delicious as the pastries were in Paris, there was a certain kind of American store-bought pastry that she always longed for when abroad but could not find. Quite impulsively, before our holiday, I bought some of these pastries, wrapped them, and decided that I would leave them at the desk of the hotel and ask that they be delivered to her.

Soon after arriving at the hotel, I made my request to the bell captain, who explained that the duke's valet was standing at the elevator and that the duke himself would soon be going out for his daily drive.

"Perhaps you would like to deliver the gift yourself. The duke enjoys a special boutonniere, a cornflower, which we keep at the desk for him. I know he'd be delighted if you gave both gifts to him personally."

The valet was informed of my presence by the bell captain, who beckoned me to join the duke at the elevator. After our introduction, I handed my gifts to the duke. He was then an old man whose face was thin and drawn. His blue eyes were translucent, somehow strangely vacant, yet still gracious—they were those of a man who had known great pain and loss.

The duke received my gifts warmly, explaining how pleased the duchess would be to receive her favorite American pastry. Because his hands trembled with age, his valet helped him to pin on his boutonniere, and after a few more minutes of conversation he shook my hand, bidding farewell.

I remember hoping, as I watched him enter his waiting limousine, that the emptiness and sadness in his eyes would go away. For I was yearning to believe that a precious love could erase all pain, even that felt by a man groomed to be king, yet in exile.

As he drove away, it was not the vision of a blissful marriage that dominated my thoughts. Instead it was the words whose import I well understood, but as yet had not the courage to face: In the real world there are no fairy tales.

✿ 33 ✿

None of us can expect to fulfill all our needs and desires, or be free from conflict, distress, and fear.

Certainly, as agonizing as it is and will be, this period of my life is teaching me how important it is to be able to wait, to plan, to work hard, to relax and have fun when possible, and to fight back when necessary in order to survive. This is so much easier because of people I know now and have known in the past who have been good to me and have loved me. There are so many kinds of love—so many. I wish in my language there were more words to express them. We have but one word—*love*—to describe so many kinds of caring. In music, the purest of languages, I can hear the types and nuances of differing loves echoed and reflected accurately and honestly.

A flood of memories rushes over me now. Sometimes love, kindness, and compassion are shared between two who do not know each other's names—I have not forgotten.

I attended elementary school in a rural area of Baltimore called Mount Washington. Though it lay within the city limits, most Baltimoreans referred to this area as "the country." Each morning the same

106

streetcar with the same driver, known affectionately by the children as the "tripper man," moved down the sparse residential area picking up all the children and taking us to our simple, happy six-room school house. And in the afternoon, the "tripper man" was always there at three o'clock to take us home.

We all adored his streetcar and regarded it as special and magical. It could be driven from the front as well as the back. In the mornings our friend used the front of his "tripper" to drive us to school, and in the afternoon, he used the back part to take us up the streetcar tracks to where each of us lived.

We had moved to Mount Washington when I was six. My father, wanting to please my mother, had bought another house—one that was miles from our old neighborhood with its endless rows of houses and their gleaming white marble steps. What neither of my parents, so young then, knew—and how many of us do in our early 20s?—is that old conflicts are taken to our new neighborhoods.

During my first weeks on the tripper, my ride was lonely. I didn't know the other children and felt very isolated. To make matters worse, I needed glasses and was embarrassed to wear them. So nearsighted that I could hardly see two feet in front of me, I squinted so much trying to see that I barely opened my eyes.

Finally, one morning I decided that seeing might help. So I got on the tripper wearing my glasses (horn-rimmed—not the pink ones my mother had thought were right). It was on that brisk October morning, a Thursday I think, that the tripper man and I became friends. Amidst laughter and the shouts of "Four-eyes," he told me he was glad to see me. Then he

107

asked if I had ever noticed what one blade of grass really looked like.

Realizing that with my glasses I could actually see individual blades, I sat down smiling. I sat next to my second friend in Mount Washington, another rebel, Suzanne Addison. Her glasses were blue.

When I was in the third grade, my mother became seriously ill. She was hospitalized with severe internal bleeding and her doctors could not determine the cause of her illness. My father, sick with worry and fear, spent most of his time with her at the hospital, which did not allow any visits from children.

As usual, Rita came each day to care for me. She just arrived earlier so that my father could get to the hospital as soon as possible. And she stayed until very late at night, when he returned home.

The second day of my mother's hospitalization, I refused to get dressed and go to school. No coaxing on Rita's part would change my mind.

"The child is stubborn and obstinate," I heard my father tell Rita angrily.

"No, Mr. Charles, and you should know better," scolded Rita, whose love for me was deep and who understood everything. "She is not obstinate. She's just scared and sick from worry—like you are."

Hearing the conversation, I remembered thinking how complicated things were. I was being stubborn, as my father said, but that's because I was so scared—as Rita said.

On the third day of my mother's hospitalization, I still felt afraid to go to school. Much to our surprise that morning, the doorbell rang. Rita gave me a hug and went to answer it, nodding as if to say that she would be right back—that I really wasn't as alone as I felt.

From the front door I heard the familiar voice of the tripper man.

"Well, Rita," he said, "I just walked up the hill from the tracks because I was wondering where your little one was. This is the third day and she hasn't been down to the tripper. We all miss her."

To this day I don't understand how Rita managed it so quickly. But before I knew it she had handed my coat to the tripper man and he helped me put it on. Then he took me by the hand to the streetcar, where the other children seemed very happy to see me. As I walked the distance with my friend, I remember feeling that my mother was going to be OK. And even if she wasn't, everything could be OK again. Somebody very nice and very kind had understood and had not forgotten about me.

I was not—regardless of the passing years—to forget about him either. For every spring when I see my first blade of grass, a treasured but nameless friend with white hair and sparkling blue eyes is remembered.

And he takes the hand of the little girl who has remained a part of me.

✿ 34 ✿

What do I most want to give my children?

Love and hope—to share with me now and in later
years when they will prepare to leave me, sharing
with others who become more important. I want to
prepare them for the time when I no longer will be.

The longer I live, the more I realize all that I do not
know. The truth of silence becomes more precious, as
does the time to reflect in solitude. Just as precious is
the time to listen, to hear what another person is saying. The only thing in life that I know—the only thing
I am very sure of—is what my own life has taught me.
The only ones I can really advise are myself and sometimes, only sometimes, my children.

For I realize that it is not what I tell my children or
try to teach them that affects them in the deepest way.
Instead, it is how they view the way I live and how
they experience our relationship that makes the difference in the choices they will make in their own
lives.

I write about love in my life or the life of others
because love, concern, and human connection offer
hope. Without this hope, it is quite difficult, some-

110

times impossible, to face life, to grow from its challenges, and to refuse to be destroyed by them.

I didn't understand this very well in my youth, but one of my thesis advisers at the University of Pennsylvania predicted that some day I would understand its importance. She once wrote in a note that I still cherish:

> As you mature I know you will become a fine clinician. And life will be your best teacher. Know yourself, value yourself, be honest with yourself. And try not to run from difficult choices even when they must hurt you. In your process of facing life—in beginning what is to be begun and ending what must be ended, in taking risks when necessary—you will often feel different—alone—but you will always continue to grow. Your choices, your answers, will be yours, no one else's. But your struggle to find them and your own growth and honesty will make your life precious and vital. And the depth and quality of your work will be enhanced beyond words.

Life is easier now because I feel part of something important, something worth living for, fighting for, and sacrificing for. Yes, I am willing to go through this divorce, whatever it takes, because I know in this way I will have a better and more fulfilling life. And in turn, I hope, I will be able to give more to my children.

❧ 35 ❧

What regrets do I have?

I have many, and yet I understand that one cannot see today as clearly today as one can tomorrow. My deepest regrets involve times and situations where my choices have hurt those I love.

I am deeply sorry that my divorce has caused pain to my children. Their birth sent shock waves through me—I owe them the best of me, the best life I can give them. I want to tell them I am sorry for any pain I have caused them. Yet I know, in spite of this pain, there is much love between us, love that will remain and continue to grow.

The disruption in our lives has, in many ways, brought us closer. I know in time they will understand for themselves more of life than my words can explain. They will find their own answers, their own explanations.

When my daughters were born I felt overwhelmed at the scope of my responsibilities. I felt inadequate and unprepared, so much so that at times I was numbed with the fear that my love for them wasn't rich or good enough. Today, I feel differently. We have struggled in many ways, and there have been and will continue to be stressful moments inevitable in any mother–daughter relationship. But I am so grateful for their presence; each is beautiful in her own way. From their first moments in my arms, Kathyanne has been my heart, Elisabeth my soul. Nothing can change that.

When I feel so deeply sad that problems not of my daughters' making have caused and continue to cause them pain, I am helped as I remember Hamlet's order to Polonius: his order about the players. Each of us, I know today, is but a player. Life offers no guarantees. We are destined to do either the best we can or the best we will.

> . . . *Let them be well used, Polonius.*
>
> *My lord, I will use them according to their desert.*
>
> *God's bodykins, man, much better. Use every man after his desert and who should 'scape whipping? Use them after your own honor and dignity; the less they deserve, the more merit is in your bounty.*

And as I remember, I think of an experience with my grandmother. I was about eleven and we were in her kitchen cooking. My grandmother never used a recipe, she read no English, and cooked as she remembered watching her mother cook so many years before—so many thousands of miles away.

As we put all the ingredients for the special cake we were making, a babka, on the kitchen table, my grandmother realized that she needed more milk than she had on hand as well as cream—a special luxury. So

113

she instructed me to go to a favorite place, the corner grocery, Mr. and Mrs. Charlie's store, "Just ask Mr. Charlie to pour out two containers of his richest milk. Then hurry home. That way we can sit together and watch the cream rise. It might take a while, so we will be patient, waiting together—for cream, in time, my dearest, always rises."

❦ 36 ❦

Whoever said life is fair?

I have been remembering them all—from long ago and from today.

As I understand more fully, I see things very differently: Past and present come together, a blend of old values and new realism. I now see that my life, to a large extent, will be what I make it. I see that as my own feelings of self-respect and dignity grow, I treat myself far better than I did in years past. I have learned, too—finally and with difficulty—that in large measure the fair treatment we give ourselves, the ability to say "Enough" when our personal boundaries are intruded upon, is reflected in how others will treat us. I have also accepted that some days I will still step backward, reverting to old, nonproductive patterns of behavior. But today when I do, I see and understand. In the past, I could not.

In finding peace within, in being as fair to myself as I can possibly be, in using my potential for both happiness and fulfillment as maturely and honestly as I can, I pave the way for a life that is as fair as it can possibly be—one in which there will also be richer gifts from me to share with others.

When my life changed so radically in October 1975, I felt all possible joy had ended, never again to return. For though my intellect told me otherwise, in my heart I too, believed a woman without a man to be a nonentity. I see now that had the woman in me been functioning well, she never could have been so deceived.

I know now that in recent years an important change has been slowly occurring within me. I had, in years past, expected others, in return for my caring for them, to take care of me—to ensure my happiness and security. For I had yet to learn that regardless of how deeply she loves, a woman must take care of herself. In so many ways, especially in the early years of my marriage, I was still a little girl, one determined to be good so that I could never be left.

Today I claim my happiness as a responsibility that is mine alone. For I know that if one is fortunate, one has memories of love past and knowledge of love present. But our choices and decisions—regardless of our life-style—are ones that only we know enough to make. We are, each of us, unique. And until we grow to understand ourselves well, we cannot be truly free, truly able to make those decisions and choices which can lead to the most meaningful life possible, one lived maturely and with joy.

Of course, there is still a little girl inside of me who sometimes becomes very frightened. Though she'll never go away completely (and I wouldn't want her to, because sometimes she can be lots of fun), even she is growing up. She is helped a lot by the woman, today a healthy one, who reminds her constantly that in this wonderful, mad journey called life, we are each alone—alone to build our lives, to grow, to laugh. We are also capable of hurting, sometimes destroying, ourselves. And sadly, all of us may meet with unfairness and cruelty and injustice in our journey through life.

Above all, I see today that the truest magic in life is love. It is possible to exist without it but not to live happily. One can find love in many places, in many varying relationships, and alone, treasuring a lovely garden, an exquisite sunset, or a snow-covered field glistening in the sunlight.

We need, too, to know satisfaction in the work that we do—whatever kind of work that is and wherever it takes place. And we must be able to take time to relax, to be, to play.

Today I feel a mixture of contentment and excitement about now and about tomorrow. For the first time in my life, the pieces of the puzzle fit; I am in harmony. There is internal peace, joy, and dignity—but fear too, yes, still fear. For one cannot know what the future holds.

But even though life isn't fair and there are no easy answers, we can be fair to ourselves. We can know what we want and need for a good life, and work to achieve it in self-respect. And we can communicate those needs to those who care and who love and can be loved.

My struggle to grow and learn and share has been, is, will continue to be worth it. I see life, in spite of its pain, as a splendid adventure, and I, though I crave a harbor, am and will remain at heart an adventurer.

I feel joy and contentment, and, in spite of tears that will remain familiar—tears that are part of life's inevitable struggle and challenge—I know peace and I am happy. I am very, very happy.

Printed in the United States
6397

9 780595 137831